Sinister Wisdom 120
Spring 2021

Publisher: Sinister Wisdom, Inc.
Editor: Julie R. Enszer
Guest Editor: Vi Khi Nao
Associate Guest Editor: Amy Haejung
Graphic Designer: Nieves Guerra
Copy Editor: Amy Haejung
Board of Directors: Roberta Arnold, Tara Shea Burke, Cheryl Clarke, Julie R. Enszer, Sara Gregory, Shromona Mandal, Joan Nestle, Rose Norman, Mecca Jamilah Sullivan, Yasmin Tambiah, and Red Washburn

Front Cover Art: *Spring Blossoms* - **Artist:** Ayirani Balachanthiran
Media: Digital Painting Size: A4

Artist statement: This piece features the Sun and Moon embracing surrounded by blossoms and flowering plants. They are timeless beings who are reinterpreted infinitely into various forms of admiration across cultures. I find power in the warm love from the Sun every morning and the gentle care from the Moon at night. It's lovely to imagine them as immortal beings enjoying their time together in a serene space. Traces of celestial admiration are found throughout my artwork since I've always been interested in the cosmic unknown. I've found solace dreaming about other-wordly spaces which allow everything to be possible and exist peacefully. The allure of these giant forces as mysterious and beautiful remind me of how I first felt towards other queer women. Spending time pondering the complexities of my identity and world while painting are how I navigate these feelings.

Back Cover Art: "I Got You" - **Artist:** Whitney Romberg-Sasaki
Media: Watercolor and Ink on Paper - **Size:** 9 x 12 inches

Artist statement: A Chicago-based artist, Whitney Romberg-Sasaki creates works around themes of self love, relationships, identity, and healing through her own experiences as a queer person of color. A California native, she has also had her work featured in a variety of DIY art festivals and galleries throughout the States. In addition to her zines and illustrations, Whitney is one of the creators of *Building Communi-Tea*, a podcast that centers the experiences of Asian American millennials. To connect with Whitney, check out her instagram @whitneykittyart. "Building Communi-Tea" (Instagram:@ buildcommunitea) is available on Spotify, Apple Music, and Anchor.

SINISTER WISDOM, founded 1976

Former editors and publishers:

Harriet Ellenberger (aka Desmoines) and Catherine Nicholson (1976–1981)

Michelle Cliff and Adrienne Rich (1981–1983)

Michaele Uccella (1983–1984)

Melanie Kaye/Kantrowitz (1983–1987)

Elana Dykewomon (1987–1994)

Caryatis Cardea (1991–1994)

Akiba Onada-Sikwoia (1995–1997)

Margo Mercedes Rivera-Weiss (1997–2000)

Fran Day (2004–2010)

Julie R. Enszer & Merry Gangemi (2010–2013)

Julie R. Enszer (2013–)

Subscribe online: www.SinisterWisdom.org
Join *Sinister Wisdom* on Facebook: www.Facebook.com/SinisterWisdom
Follow *Sinister Wisdom* on Instagram: www.Instagram.com/sinister_wisdom
Follow *Sinister Wisdom* on Twitter: www.twitter.com/Sinister_Wisdom
Sinister Wisdom is a US non-profit organization; donations to support the work and distribution of *Sinister Wisdom* are welcome and appreciated. Consider including *Sinister Wisdom* in your will.

Sinister Wisdom, 2333 McIntosh Road, Dover, FL 33527-5980 USA

TABLE OF CONTENTS

NOTES FOR A MAGAZINE

When I was a young reader, a number of iconic lesbian and feminist anthologies did vital identity formation work for me—and for women broadly. I think of anthologies such as *The Tribe of Dina* (first published as *Sinister Wisdom* 29/30) *Nice Jewish Girls*, *This Bridge Called My Back*, *Conditions: Five / The Black Woman's Issue*, *Chicana Lesbians: The Girls Our Mothers Warned Us About*, and many more. These books were central to my thinking about what it meant to be a lesbian in the world.

Lesbian journals have long been vital spaces where we think about and through the varied meanings of multiple identities. *Sinister Wisdom* has been a crucial site for this activity historically with issues focused on identity elaboration including *A Gathering of Spirit* (Sinister Wisdom 22/23), *The Tribe of Dina*, *Tellin' It Like It Is* (Sinister Wisdom 47), and *Latina Lesbians* (Sinister Wisdom 74), and these gestures have continued under my editorship.

In this tradition, I am thrilled to publish *Sinister Wisdom* 120: *Asian Lesbians*. Vi Khi Nao has assembled a terrific array of writing by Asian lesbians that invites vibrant thinking about the meaning of lesbian among Asian-American lesbians, lesbians in Asia, and throughout the Asian diaspora. It is thrilling to have so much amazing writing gathered in one place, and as often happens with these types of projects, *Sinister Wisdom* 120: *Asian Lesbians* is an especially chunky issue.

I am also aware of a delicate balance for *Sinister Wisdom* to maintain. We want to have issues devoted to identity elaborations and also to ensure that, as a multicultural journal, all of our issues are thinking critically about racial-ethnic identities and other social-political identities within these pages. We want to create vibrant spaces with important conversations where everyone can "listen in" to key questions within communities, and we want to create spaces that are in conversation with questions of race and ethnicity even when not named on the cover. Let me know how you think we are doing on this balance.

As always in this April issue of *Sinister Wisdom*, I want to thank everyone who supported our fall fundraiser which was successful this year as it has been in all years where I've been working on the journal. Thank you to everyone who stepped up to make a donation, give a gift subscription, and otherwise extend the reach of *Sinister Wisdom* and help us make our publish work possible in 2021. Thank you also to everyone who has joined in our zoom events. We have been trying to lean into this moment of the Covid-19 pandemic and the extraordinary political situation in the United States calling us to witness new calls for racial justice and new challenges to our democratic system. Casey Moore stepped up mid-pandemic to help coordinate our online events, and I have relied on her for lots of different events. Thank you, Casey, for your leadership and your skills in helping us operate online. Also, thank you to Cassidy Scanlon who has made our visual life in the email newsletter and online even more beautiful. Thank you to the entire *Sinister Wisdom* board of directors who each work individually to help make the journal be its very best. And thank you, dear readers, for reading and tuning in to all of our conversations, and for joining us in celebrating lesbian imaginations.

In sisterhood,

Julie R. Enszer, PhD
Editor and Publisher

NOTES FOR A SPECIAL ISSUE

Vi Khi Nao

I was in my late twenties when I first saw Deepa Mehta's *Fire*. It was the first Asian lesbian film, I felt, that wasn't designed for and catered to the male Western penis. I grew up in Long Khánh, Vietnam, near a forest of rubber trees and coffee beans, earth so red it could dye my young legs into red envelopes worthy of handing out during Tết, and a flea-infused tropical climate that forced us to have practical relationships with mosquito nets. During the tender sapphic lovemaking scene between the two leads, Sita and Radha, Deepa Mehta has naturally endorsed that such intimacy be choreographed in the unelevated atmosphere of a mosquito-netted bedchamber. The scene struck a powerful chord in my Asian carnal consciousness. In part because I grew up in Vietnam, whose rurality was so romantic I had no choice but to love that which is simple and sensible. The sapphic tenderness between Sita and Radha changed the primary landscape of my desire and continues to impact me and my literary work. Most of the sapphic lovemaking scenes I see in cinema, in art, and in literature have very little to do with mosquito nets. Instead, they take place on sofas, kitchen tables, carpeted floors—none such household furniture ever spoke directly to my Asian desire. They speak the general language of desire, but as most of you know, generality leads to more generality—and desire doesn't operate well under a one-size-fits-all regime. There is erotic isolation that an Asian queer individual endures when the capsulation of desire has been exported or transplanted elsewhere and has been fitted for mass consumption.

Since the relatively recent births of a few dozen Asian lesbian films, for instance a few South Korean delights such as Park Chan-wook's *The Handmaiden* and Lee Hyun-ju's *Our Love Story*, visibility for Asian lesbians has augmented gradually, slowly, sluggishly, and sometimes anxiously. I say anxiously because each year, I never know if I will ever see a great Asian film again, as if I were anxious about an imminent queer apocalypse in Asian lesbian cinema, meaning, Asian lesbians viewers would be eating canned rice and mung beans, or whatever soft porn YouTube channels would deliver, and nothing else for decades and even millennia to come. Our desire would be decimated or curated by Western porn industries designed for white male consumers. As for literature, I haven't read a single book that addresses the depth of Asian sapphic desire in a way that speaks to my heart tenderly, prodigiously, erotically, linguistically, emotionally. Most of my desire, on appearance, has been borrowed from the West; I wish for something I could call ethnically my own. "Borrowed" because I have primarily read queer books by white authors such as Jeanette Winterson, Carole Maso, and Sarah Waters (from whose famous *Fingersmith* Park Chan-wook drew his inspiration for *The Handmaiden*).

It goes without saying that some of what we consume, and therefore produce, will have an overarching influence from Western cultures, canons, and aesthetics. How could it not? Perhaps I grew up in the Midwest for too long (over twenty years), thinking I was the only Asian lesbian in the world. Even my favorite dish—just plain white rice or jasmine rice—has the word "white" in it. Thus, the influence of the West is an inevitable reality—linguistically, carnally, artistically, gastronomically— on most (if not all) work by Asian lesbians. Even deeply loved, popular Vietnamese cuisine such as phở and bánh mì have some of their culinary legs in French history. So I am more than thrilled to say that in this curated anthology, Asian queer artists, writers, poets, entrepreneurs, filmmakers, designers, and Instagrammers have surprised me with the strength, breadth, and depth of their "Asianness"—whatever that is. Even if some of the work does not, on first glance, appear very Asian, each piece has its arms and legs squarely in Asian sapphic aesthetics, whatever that is, also. I want to give you some shape or sense of how this collection came to be born. When *Sinister Wisdom* first put out its call for an Asian lesbian anthology, there weren't many submissions. Perhaps the venues we chose for our calling did not hit the right demographics. The limited submissions sent me into a panic mode. I was led on by my own misperception that perhaps there were truly no Asian lesbians, let alone in the arts. So, to fatten the collection, I started interviewing all of the writers, poets, artists, filmmakers, performance artists, restaurant owners, etc. who were accepted for publication. Three or four months in, *Sinister Wisdom* was able to disseminate the call more broadly; we began to receive an overload of submissions and I began to pull back on the interviews. Finally, due to the quantity of submissions, I stopped interviewing altogether. If you wonder why some contributors were interviewed and others weren't, the answer is quite simple: I interviewed whoever submitted during the first round. I am grateful that that initial, unjustified panic gave me the opportunity to explore in depth works by marvelous contributors such as, to name a few, Sri Lankan, Tamil-born, raised-in-New-York visual artist Ayirani Balachanthiran; South Korean–born, New Jersey–adopted artist, Mi Ok Song; and Los Angeles–based interdisciplinary artist Sydney S. Kim.

The contributions here are, as you can see, from a vast range of queer Asians (artists from all facets, modalities, genres of existence). I hope they will represent some of your desires, if not all, and speak to your Asian hearts in ways that other anthologies haven't. This anthology is designed to be highly ambitious, all-encompassing and inclusive, tender and provocative, experimental and cliché, fragile and resilient, vulnerable and hardcore, dynamic and demonstrative, embarrassing and awkward, perfect and incomplete, tantalizing and boring, garrulous and reticent, overwhelming and microscopic, cosmic and delirious, emotional and cephalic, erotic and mundane, and mostly Asian and female and queer and specific, just for you. I want this anthology to make you feel less isolated in your desire. To experience the beauty and vulnerability and depth of talent from all over the world and to know that your art, your desire, your Asianness has a home and is validated. When I lived in Iowa for over twenty years, I thought I was the only Asian lesbian in the world; your submissions and contributions have altered my misperception. Now, I feel less alone in my yearning for women. Now, I feel less alone in my Asianness. Your courage and openness have changed this for me. And I hope that this anthology, despite its imperfection and incompleteness, will serve, at the very least, as a throat clearing for your own journey with desire, your connection with this intimate community, and your ever-changing relationship with Asian culture, art, poetry, fiction, and cinema in the years to come.

—VI KHI NAO, Las Vegas, May 2020

MY NAME MEANS GODDESS

Shivani Dave

My Name Means Goddess

my hips learned to speak in Kathak classes
praising goddesses who were set on fire, but never burned
my too small kid lips painted red hot
before i could master the grace of lipstick
my hands balanced scenes of Natarajan's triumph over evil,
thighs thundered in rhythm with Krishna chasing Leela
my body swayed in motion with
Rama freeing Sita from her demons
I rehearsed resilience
but not all conquest is choreographed
ripped at the seams, my hips
bucked against yours pleads
just for a second, one
two sometimes recognition is obscured by
three promises of love, maybe that's why
four I am still counting, four every time I am on my knees
I feel your grip force yourself between my hips
five I find femme rage burning in the Hindu myths memorized
by my fingertips
one In Kali who collects the heads she severs around her neck
two In Parvati who splits herself into ten, one to answer every
doubt of her strength
three In Durga who built an impenetrable fortress for femme devotion
four, I find Shakti in Shivani, in telling the stories of my hips
and I've prayed to myself every night since

SOMETHING THAT

Shivani Dave

color me something that chokes
rageful screams of pleasure out of me, hide it
in the way you say my name
color me something that bleeds
outside the lines
deep blue sea, not red like
blood that breathes
but blood that boils underneath something that reads
not that surface level shit.
i am writing for soft skin armor taught something that races, color me
speed lightning rain
drops that drag me by the waist
to chase the puddles pacing
at our feet, release me
from a cerebral state of plain,
color me something that punches
arrows straight and narrow
fists that fit in small spaces
squirm beyond encasement
against restrain, repeat this refrain
until i am undisguised tongue tied
around curvaceous praises searing reclamation!
then
color me something that drips
exhale across my ridges
each heave brings me to my knees
so that i can—
breathe

DEAR WOMEN WHO ARE NOT EMBARRASSED WHEN THEIR NIPPLES GET HARD IN PUBLIC,

Jax NTP

did you know that deserts are the first place to thirst
because they were the ancient oceans that dried first

evolution of consciousness and totems for a sea witch
nautilus, squid, cuttlefish, octopus locomotion defense

i haven't been able to process joy since i've inherited
my mother's trauma while she was pregnant with me

it is easier to thread the needle if you lick it first, mother
taught me feminine etiquette at a young age i had to let go

erect motion and bait, a simple love story in three parts
cut the deck and draw the strength, trilobite transformations

con không được yêu đàn bà

tell me about all the things we can't undo
threats are promises people want to keep

at some point, you cannot live in rage, stop fighting
to allow yourself a chance to heal, go on, draw the three of cups

LET'S MAKE A LIST OF WOMEN IN POWER NOW

Jax NTP

the trees are so still they are about to catch on fire
we wake up for something to do someone to become
the difference between aria and warble invisible red

an expression of empathy is to classify pain
what does it mean if top five is the only five
the unexpected happiness when the RN asks

us to rate our physical level of pain
on a scale from familiar to alien
what we know when top five is the only five

as in *not us* a circular stiffness limbs asleep
what happens to a poem of resistance left unread
classification as erasure as caged caught

the expected happiness of our next shift nurse
the opportunity to offer self again weigh in flux
tinted hyacinth tainted feminine soiled not phallic

how to file the unknown
        how to file
                how to un-know

JURY ASSEMBLY ROOM, WESTMINSTER, CA

Jax NTP

the sun cooks dirt onto the park bench
when did opting out become so alluring liberation

from responsibility means to be excused from fault
but isn't fallibility a form of sandpaper
even if there isn't any actual sand used?

book idea for sale: how to navigate the world as an anxious
immigrant queer using only hypothetical scenarios

indecision cannot be attractive because all we do
all we ever wanted to do was the right thing chosen

to be inducted   opting in   glass abrasions
the sun cooks death off the park bench

IN CONVERSATION WITH VI KHI NAO

Jax NTP

VI KHI NAO: How has your day been, Jax? Have you been teaching? What are you like as a teacher? Are you a martinet? Or soft like a cheesecake?

JAX NTP: Excellent, I just gave a final exam for my summer course: Freshman Composition, ten weeks. As a teacher, I am flexible with necessary deadlines. That's a funny answer.

VKN: What is an unnecessary deadline?

JN: Well, colleges are moving toward the idea of not grading or using a "simple" pass / no pass system to deconstruct the traditional structure of grading and deadlines. Deans and department heads want instructors to be more aware of students' ongoing anxiety and "affective" issues that they have to deal with outside of the classroom. All this is to say, removing the idea of deadlines. I'm rambling.

VKN: What do you think of that system? Do you welcome it?

JN: I acknowledge the positive reinforcements and encouraging aspects of the movements toward a new system where we question the idea of how we used to teach. But at the same time, I do see the benefit of using college deadlines as a soft practice to excel in any field post-graduation.

VKN: One of your poems has a provocative title: "let's make a list of women in power now." If you were to make a less enigmatic list, who would you put on it?

JN: All the women running for the Democratic Party right now. But part of the enigmatism of it is that I was unable to clearly make one.

VKN: When I first started reading your poem "dear women who are not embarrassed when their nipples get hard in public," I felt like I was casually though not sexually strolling through your words, minding my own business, and suddenly I read this line: "con không được yêu đàn bà." It startled me at first because instead of seeing a tree, it felt more like a porcupine jumped out at me. I usually don't expect Vietnamese words to wander around in the literary backyard of America. I am curious, though—why did you decide to insert such a covert Vietnamese diacritical moment in a landscape of English words? Also, I wonder why you use women "đàn bà" in place of other gender-connoting words such as "con gái" or "công chúa." When I think of the word "đàn bà," I think of a sexless woman who walks around the world caning inanimate objects in search of her nonexistent "eve" which is the opposite of herself.

JN: I love this question—you are such a thoughtful reader. I've been playing with titles in my current project. I play with the idea of title, first line, and last line in how they are able to generate their own aside or story when read independent of the poem. In this current project, I challenge myself to play with the stream of consciousness as ropes and double-dutching. The concept of a speaker who is interrupted in a poem, however—the reader is left uncertain if a line of Vietnamese command comes from the speaker themselves or if their thoughts are being interrupted by the culture's social norms. I meant to use the word "đàn bà" in reference to the gender as a whole, whereas the words "con gái" or "công chúa" provoke a softer yet more loving connotation to the person in reference. But I'm not sure if it came across that way. Three to four years ago, I kept my identity quite separate from the work that I produced because I was struggling with labels. Now, I realize that is silly because it is impossible, at least for me, to compartmentalize myself that way as a writer.

VKN: What is your favorite word in Vietnamese? In general, and/or for terms of endearment?

JN: I can narrow it down to three: nếu (denotation: if; connotation for me: possibility), thiết tha (denotation: earnest; connotation for me: yearning), nước mắt (denotation: tears; connotation for me: water from eyes). A term of endearment that I've never used but would like to use one day: Người Yêu Ơi (I don't know how to translate that! Can you help? Person I love, where are you?).

VKN: This may seem non-sequitur, but have you ever dated another Vietnamese "đàn bà" before? I have not . . . and I have been wanting to (eventually), just so I know. I always find the endearing words such as "em ơi" a little bit too sisterly, and it's hard walking around the world calling người yêu ơi casually. For comedic reasons, sure. Do you feel that Vietnamese language should invent another word for our so-called or desired đồng tình luyến ái nữ? If so, what word would that be?

JN: I have not dated another Vietnamese "đàn bà"—whoa—and I feel that this says something about me. When I was in middle school, a boyish Chinese classmate gave me a note and referred to herself as "anh" and to me as "em," and I didn't understand but wasn't upset. Until my mother found the note, and then it was clear at twelve that pronouns and references to me are not as solid as what my family are comfortable with. Yes! I feel that the Vietnamese language currently doesn't have the words to fully encapsulate love for gay people. I have toyed with the idea of using "người yêu," which in my head translates to "the person I love." Unfortunately, although it feels/sounds more inclusive, there's an odd formally that makes it not intimate to use. On a different note, I feel the phrase "đồng tình luyến ái nữ" (at least when I was a child) is used to describe desire in such a negative/yuck state of mind. It reads biological, or like a bad weather report when heard on the radio or news. Perhaps we need to reclaim it. Ha!

VKN: It's funny that you found "đồng tình luyến ái nữ" too meteorological. I found it incredibly Shakespearean. Like sexuality in Vietnamese, the word "việt kiều" sounds baroque and over-ornamented, which feels in alignment with Vietnam's colorful texture and liveliness. To contrast this, the last stanza of your poem has this wise epiphany: "at some point, you cannot live in rage." Can you speak a little about the source of this line? How did it come to you?

JN: It is a rough translation of or loose reference to a tarot reading I had done for myself. In this poem, readers get to loosely interact with the Major Arcana Strength card and the three of cups. When I completed the reading, I was sure it wasn't working. But in hindsight, I was simply unaware of my anger because I have simply been living with it. There's also a quote I really like: "Holding on to anger is like grasping a hot coal with the intent of harming another; you end up getting burned." Maybe a part of me wished to write the anger away.

VKN: Can you talk a little about your relationship to park benches? They were mentioned twice in one poem. I suspected that jury duty and bench and park bench share legal/public spaces. It moves from its nascent opening "the sun cooks dirt" to its enclosure "the sun cooks death"—can you speak about your thoughts behind this poem's evolutionary, metaphorical leap? Is there quantum logic there?

JN: I wrote that poem within fifteen minutes on a literal park bench outside the courthouse post–jury duty. I was upset then, because after sitting around for four to five hours, I was stipulated during jury process because I had identified as queer. The irony of being out and being afraid vs. being out and unable to serve because you are out. I think my poetic leap play, with first line and last line repetition here, nods at the idea that no matter what legal restrictions cook up to cook queer people out, in the end we all die. I didn't feel evolutionary when I wrote it; it felt like more of a (un)settling realization.

VKN: I am sorry that happened to you! No wonder you were upset. I would be too. When did you know that you were queer? Lesbian? Or bê đê to make it less about climate change. And do you know of any Vietnamese films or books that reflect your desire?

JN: I didn't know until my first girlfriend told me. I didn't have the words or wasn't able to identify with the words "lesbian" and "queer" until the beginning of college. In hindsight, I always knew, because everything that was happening around me in the Vietnamese or American schools that I attended—I didn't quite fit into the idea of any young adult girl fantasies about weddings and boys.

VKN: I love how your poems appear to have "predictable" or "suggestive" titles—but as readers navigate through your work, they discover there are hidden and forbidden insights waiting to be the opposite of feminine etiquettes, providing depth to the poem's deceivingly simple foregrounding. Do titles arrive to you before their bodies have been written? Or do they come in tandem?

JN: For the last couple of years, a title has earned its place after it has been haunting me for weeks. Sometimes a title is a favorite line from a previous poem that needed a new life. This goes back to the idea of double-dutching: a form of braiding narratives in my epistolary collection.

VKN: What is the best lesbian film you have ever seen? And, why do you love it so much?

JN: Oh no. My three favorites: *The Hours*, *Saving Face*, and *Kissing Jessica Stein*. I've been criticized before for these titles, but they have highly rewatchable qualities for me.

VKN: And your favorite poet? And why were you criticized?

JN: Gertrude Stein, because she defamiliarizes the familiar and the banal to create new meaning. She uses repetition to challenge/unsettle basic concepts. Her writing is both political and playful. I was criticized for my favorite movies because they are not artsy enough or not queer enough or represent too much of a straight gaze into queer identities. But the pickings are slim.

VKN: I love her too. She seems to be very good at making up endearing terms (terms I wouldn't want to be called) for her Alice B. Toklas. By the way, what does NTP mean?

JN: I used to not share what NTP meant. But I think I have grown. Really, it is just the rest of my name in Vietnamese: Nhã Thanh Phạm. It is too feminine, and because my mother said I failed to live up to the softness and etherealness of the name, I am shy about it without wanting to ditch it completely, so I abbreviated it.

VKN: I suspected that may be the case! You have a beautiful name! Excellent for a poet! I do understand your sense of diffidence and reservation about it. Perhaps give it some time. I don't think it's that feminine. It reminds me more of the fruit: longan (nhãn). Have you had dinner? What will you eat tonight?

JN: I'm going to celebrate before diving into grading final papers. I'm craving spicy roasted duck panang curry with lychee and grapes. We shall see if I can make the trip out to get some.

RHYTHM

Naina Ayya

Watercolor and ink

QUEER LOST LOVE

Jessica Nguyen

how do I say
"I love you"
when what I was was barely taught to say it to my parents

when what you want to hear
is a love that is
not of a chị thương em (familial) but a chị yêu em (romantic)

and so
I said nothing
but watch the sun rise and disappear in your eyes I've done you
wrong for not releasing the words that would allow you to exist
in my life

IN CONVERSATION WITH VI KHI NAO

Jessica Nguyen

VI KHI NAO: Are you a fan of 3 a.m.? 9 p.m.? What is your relationship to those precise hours/markers?

JESSICA NGUYEN: I used to be a complete night owl. Sometimes I would work on my passion projects until 5 a.m. in the morning routinely, so 3 a.m. would sound pretty normal to me at that time. My previous evening job allowed me to have that type of schedule. Nowadays, though, I've been sticking more to the earlier hours. I've been working at three different Vietnamese restaurants (currently on a work and holiday visa in Australia) and all of them close at 10 p.m. So, 9 p.m. is like, "Oh, it's almost time for home to relax and Netflix!" I don't sleep until much later. I guess you can say that I just never sleep!

VKN: In some of your nonprofit, charitable work, you have translated Vietnamese to English and vice versa. Do you ever feel that these translations are an extension of your poetry? Like an ice sculptor sculpting cultural, figurative, lyrical ice in the middle of spring, knowing full well that the work will not preserve and will melt in little time? Or do you think that poetry carves a different space in a writer's consciousness, such as there is a time for life and then there is time for poetry?

JN: I have always found Vietnamese to be poetic but never considered using it as part of my poetry until recently. I speak Vietnamese often enough on a day-to-day basis to not see Vietnamese translations as an extension of my poetry. These translations are inherently necessary as they will most likely come up in my daily thoughts and conversations. I think and speak in both English and Vietnamese fluently.

When I write poetry, I use language that's more direct and forward with the imagery that I'm trying to create, because I find that being practical with my word choice allows me to be honest with who I am.

VKN: Can you walk us through your poem? When did you write it? And, how long did it take you to write it? Do you believe in poetic epiphanies?

JN: I started writing in my middle school years in a personal blog (which was when a lot of us became angsty teenagers). I started collecting pieces of my writing gradually. All I knew at that time was that I enjoyed writing. I struggled with articulating a lot of my thoughts when I was younger, so writing was my way of trying to piece together what I wanted to say but couldn't. I don't stick to a hard deadline when it comes to writing (didn't work out when I tried to).

I use writing as a medium to express feelings that I felt like I couldn't share with anybody else at that time. There were words left unspoken for the person I had feelings for. "queer lost love" was one of those moments when writing became a healing experience for me. I wrote this piece a few weeks before this interview, because I was reflecting on a time in my life that I realized I never gave myself the opportunity to process and let go.

Usually, I just write when I feel like it, so I really do believe in poetic epiphanies. And writing poetry is faster when you're in the mood, you know? My latest epiphany that's been helping me write a lot more is incorporating Vietnamese in my poems, simply because I feel like there's so much packed into my parents' language that hasn't been explored yet. I have a very deep relationship with my home culture, and writing in Vietnamese draws out a very important piece of history that makes up me and where I come from.

VKN: If you could invent a word in Vietnamese to express the love between two women, what word would that be? This is in response to the second stanza of your poem, "queer lost love." To quote you: "[not of a chị thương em (familial) but a chị yêu em (romantic)]." I have always felt really awkward saying, vocalizing endearing terms in Vietnamese with my sapphic lovers because I found no equivalent words in the Vietnamese language to express the feminine tenderness I possess for my same-sex lovers. Don't you feel that the word "chị" has a way of incestualizing this female homoerotic very much? Doesn't it make you cringe? And "em yêu em" exudes narcissism, not just sonically. As if Vietnamese, the language, is homophobic and emotional and linguistically perverse by nature. At least for Vietnamese dykes and lesbians. For men (anh và em), I think the language is more tender and fluid and almost captivatingly adorable.

JN: Yes! I always feel awkward trying to figure out which pronouns to use when I'm speaking to someone in Vietnamese. I understand the need to show respect to older people in our culture, but I feel like some parts of our language—for example, pronouns—inhibit us from feeling comfortable with expressing ourselves to others in more intimate ways. And I agree with you on how the Vietnamese language seems inherently homophobic and I wouldn't be surprised if there are people out there who argue that because there are not many words used to identify the queer community, we don't exist.

I would feel very uncomfortable confessing my love to someone using "chị," because I have a younger sister and I wouldn't love her in that way. "Chị" and "em" are usually used to establish a familial connection with other people, even if they're not blood-related. So, to me, I definitely get goosebumps when I imagine myself awkwardly vocalizing "I love you" in Vietnamese.

I've thought of using the gender-neutral and hierarchy-neutral alternative "mình yêu bạn," but the connotations behind the pronouns are very different. They're used for more formal situations when we don't know the other person very well and we want to be polite to them, so using "mình" and "bạn" immediately creates a distance between the giver and recipient, which doesn't feel appropriate for something so emotional and heartfelt like a romantic confession.

I wouldn't be surprised to hear that a lot of heterosexual men find it easy to express themselves in their relationships either, because many languages are very patriarchal and made for these cis-heterosexual men.

If I could invent a word in Vietnamese, it would sound very close to "mến," which is often used "yêu mến," but "mến" on its own means to hold someone dearly and I like the idea of holding my partner as someone dear to me.

VKN: What is it like working for three Vietnamese restaurants? What are the restaurants like? Do they serve tàu hủ nóng at all? Do you love to cook? Would you ever eat tàu hủ nóng while driving a moped in New York City? Near MOMA, possibly?

JN: I work from 11 a.m. to 11 p.m. at two of the restaurants and these two are very traditional Vietnamese establishments. Their menus have hundreds of the same food items and there's not as much focus on decorating the interior. Chefs are known to work in the kitchen during open hours. These chefs are usually the ones who own and manage the restaurants as well if they're not a franchise, so they have their own very particular ways of running the business. I've learned to appreciate the systems that have been established in the restaurants by generations of waiters and other workers who have come before me. There's a lot of thought and carefulness that take place not just in the cooking but in the prep and interaction with customers.

The third restaurant that I work at, which is a modern Vietnamese banh mi shop founded by my Vietnamese-Australian millennial friend (shout out to Shop Bao Ngoc!), proves that this emphasis on being mindful in everything that we do can be passed down. We've had hours of discussion about how food has impacted us as the Vietnamese diaspora and how we as the younger generation are trying to translate our history with Vietnamese food with a more modern take for future generations to come.

Visiting Vietnamese restaurants outside Vietnam definitely brings me back to my childhood. On my weekends in Chicago, my parents would always take me to this one restaurant on Broadway Avenue for a bowl of phở bò viên as a reward for putting up with the hours of grocery shopping and laundry labor. I feel like Vietnamese restaurants in Australia are the same as the ones in the US, which is a very comforting feeling for me since I'm living thousands of miles away from everyone and every place I call home. I am starting to enjoy cooking more at my current base because of my being so close to food very often at work and my partner's love for cooking.

Oh, and tàu hủ nóng is more seen as a behind-the-scenes treat for workers at my restaurant. I would eat tàu hủ nóng on a moped in NYC on a cold, wintery day (near MOMA if I was invited to a photoshoot that would be used to promote Vietnamese cuisine). I think we need more of these Vietnamese foodie life hacks to survive the bitter cold in the US—this is partially why I'm in Australia, ha-ha.

VKN: I was reading your Instagram posts in preparation for this interview. I noticed that you have traveled widely—all over the world, actually. Of the places you have been (Korea, Iceland, Vietnam, of course, etc.), which place feels the most Vietnamese, outside of Vietnam, or most "homoerotically" comfortable or accepting for you, if there is such a thing? Or for any Vietnamese person in general? They say California is fairly progressive, but I feel it's not that progressive and I do not feel at home, at times, sapphically there.

JN: I feel like Australia, the country I'm currently living in, has made me feel the most Vietnamese since I left the States. I think it's partially because Australia is geographically closer to Vietnam, and besides California, I've never seen so many Vietnamese businesses in different pockets of the area before! I also want to mention that I live in Melbourne, which is a much more culturally rich region than other cities in Oz.

In terms of spaces that are most homoerotically comfortable for me, I always gravitate toward those that host spoken word events. Funnily enough, in every country I've lived in, I've always felt the safest and the most myself in niche spaces that appeal to Asian artists and activists. It's these spaces that have inspired me to get into writing more recently as well.

VKN: Of all of your poems and aphorisms you have produced over the years, which piece of yours do you find yourself frequently returning to? And what about it allows you to cope with the future (your younger wiseself guiding the future, anxious self, for instance)?

JN: I've read "quiet" to the public several times. This piece was a milestone for me as it was the one that pushed me to want to be seen and heard in front of a crowd. "quiet" spoke to my racial awakening and how it implicitly describes the relationship I have with my identity as an Asian American. It serves as a reminder for myself to acknowledge and honor my journey as a Vietnamese hyphenated American.

VKN: Do you have a favorite Vietnamese word? And what do you think of this "compound" literary combo "âu yếm"—and if you were to translate that word into English, for instance, without resorting to memory or dictionary, just based on the sound of it or on what it provokes deep inside you, how would you translate it?

JN: My favorite Vietnamese word is "thương," which is actually the very word that I incorporated into "queer lost love" (even though it did not make a fitting word for what I was looking to express my feelings with). Meanings get lost in translation, and I find that the word "thương" is often misinterpreted. If I had to translate it in English, I would stick it between "love" and care about"—though I'm not very satisfied with how I'm categorizing it, either . . .

"Thương" is like a love that *can* be romantic *but* more familial, and connotes a deeper, more genuine connection that's emanating from the feeler. "Thương" is innocent, pure, raw, wholesome, honest love. But because it's often used in a familial context, the romantic appeal of its use gets overshadowed and lost.

When I hear "âu yếm," I automatically cringe—not in an "ew, I don't want that" way (though I can understand how some would associate the word with that overbearing effect), but just as a neutral physical reaction to it. Like, in an "okay, I'm cute; hold me" kind of way. To me, I feel like I'm reacting to how the saying of the word would expect me to react. I think it's interesting to see how people like my sister and me would react to this word differently. I think our different reactions reflect our history with the users of this word (most likely our parents and other adults in the family) and our relationship with our bodies and the concept of intimacy.

VKN: The word "thương" also connotes "wound" like as in vết thương and/or pity. This word has always appeared as agony or pain/painful for me, a love that is filled with aches and regrets. How do you remove the pain from that word when said in context to love? Speaking of ache, have you always known that you were queer? What was that journey like, Jessica?

JN: Yeah! I wasn't very conscious about how "thương" can appear to be a more painful kind of love until you brought it up. I grew up hearing "thương" from my parents and grandparents who have been through a lot of adversities to be able to not just to survive, but to live as well. In my eyes, they survived war and tragedy to be able to love in life. They are able to say "ba mẹ thương con" or "ông bà thương con" because they fought for love. I could never be more grateful for what they've done for me. They suffered a lot, choosing to come out with battle wounds so that their children would be left unmarked.

I didn't always know that I was queer. I still am closeted to my parents, but I am close enough to my parents to ask random hypothetical questions like, "What if your child was gay?" Interestingly enough, my mother and father had very different reactions to each other. They were basically on opposite ends of the spectrum—from "Oh, that's fine as long as you can take of yourself after your college graduation," to "I would cry endlessly; why are you asking this?"

I don't think I would've been as open to the idea that I could be queer if I hadn't gone to such a liberal women's college like Smith College. There were so many attractive women there! It's like, how can you *not* daydream about them as romantic partners?

My first crush at Smith was a close woman friend of mine. She's also the inspiration behind "queer lost love." We're still good friends to this day, but I'm sure that she isn't aware of my past feelings for her at all.

I haven't fully come out to my parents yet and I don't feel the need to, either. The media hypes up coming out as if it's a must-do coming-of-age chapter in life, but unless I'm marrying a woman, I don't intend to come out to them anytime soon. I'm not ready open that Pandora's box yet.

VKN: Do your parents/siblings/family know about your queerness? What have their responses been like? Do your parents have certain expectations for you?

JN: Only my sister knows about my queerness. It took her awhile to process because my coming out was also a surprise for her. We grew up fawning over our crushes on guys we knew in our life more.

My parents don't know that I'm queer, but like every traditional Vietnamese parent, my mom expects me to marry a cis-heterosexual man.

VKN: Did it make you feel closer to your sister when you came out? What do you think of sheep, Jessica? Have you ever ridden (written? possibly?) on a buffalo before? Would you ever have one in a backyard in Chicago?

JN: We're already very close to begin with, so I wasn't worried about my coming out to her. I trust that she will accept me regardless of who I choose to love.

Well, that's a random question! I would like to lie my head on one if it doesn't kill me. Their fur is so seemingly soft and warm that it reminds me of this blanket that I constantly bring around the house because of how easily I get cold. For some reason, it would be seventy degrees Fahrenheit outside and I would still find it chilly, so having a transportable sheep to âu yếm with would be nice. I guess that's why wool products are so great.

I've never ridden or written on a buffalo, but I would if someone dared me to do it for a bowl of bún bò Huế or cơm hến from Huế, the origin city of these two dishes. However, I would not have one in my backyard; it would be too sad for the buffalo. There are enough souls who are living far away from their home.

VKN: Your soul has traversed through and dabbled in different vectors of art (fashion and photography) and continues to. Which discipline (one in which you haven't dabbled) would you find appealing ten years down the road? For instance, would you ever pursue acting? Or ballet? Or something else entirely?

JN: I don't let myself be tied to one project. Like you said, I've had the privilege of dabbling in many vectors of art in my past and will continue to do so until my last breath. Although I feel like I'm just getting started with writing and fashion—a chapbook and a clothing line are currently in the works—I would love to explore acting more in the future. Based on what a friend of mine has witnessed so far, she's pointed out to me that I've been a performer for many of the projects that I've worked on—from modeling for my fashion blog to hosting on the Project Voice podcast to reading my poetry onstage in front of an audience. So, who knows? Maybe one day, I'll act!

TORN.

S.L. Clarke

you held my hand
as we walked along the street
you took me to that little corner,
you know the one . . .
where we'd eat 石河子凉皮.
although it's gone now,
the memory still remains,
unfaded.

it's funny how things changed.
you pointed at them and said:
look there's some 拉拉.
you told me how
they couldn't get married,
and how their parents disowned them.

you told me how
they had to hide away from society,
how so many talked as if they were trash.
but in the world through your eyes,
all women were trash, anyway.

but you know,
i thought they were so vibrant,
unlike the gray world i lived in . . .
they looked genuinely happy,
full of color.

because they weren't accepted,
they were completely content,

because they had to create
their own world
in which to exist,
just the two of them.

i readily admit,
in that moment,
i was drowned in
a pure, untainted admiration . . .
perhaps it was envy—
they had all to themselves
everything i had ever wanted
my life to be.
but, it wasn't.

now i'm back in the states,
but i'm no longer yours.
i could no longer be silent,
in the violence you called your culture,
a culture which is now a part of me,
听话,
evermore.

no more broken glasses,
shattered bowls, and plates;
no more slamming doors,
smashing through walls,
no more hospital stays.

here,
i'm stuck between two worlds.
somewhere between east and west,
is this the meaning of ethnicity?
authenticity?

because lately,
it certainly feels like i'm undefined.
飘飘的,
floating.
free falling fast,
sinking,
bloating.
but certainly a lover of women,
i am.

no more permissions,
especially on big decisions.
i'm my own to keep, now.

i'm not sure,
but I think I'm on
a permanent sex vacation,
honestly, i'm enjoying it.
. . . is that okay?

CLEO

Ali Raz

Someone calls me cute. I blush and believe her.

*

This person's name is Cleo. She's studying finance and stripping on the side. Months after our encounter, I continue to dream of her.

*

She tells me I can't touch her. Then she smiles, *That's how they get you to pay for the Champagne Room.*
Her cunt is inches from my face.

*

I send her a postcard. I omit no details. I know these postcards never reach her.

*

There's a film about strippers that was filmed in Tribeca.
I have never been to Tribeca.
I hate Manhattan, which they call, with such delusion, The City.

*

Once I sat in Dumbo and watched a fireworks display. It would have been magnificent on any other occasion, but that day it had rained, and was still drizzling, and the ground was wet, and the fireworks seemed to fizzle against the sky, which all day had been eating the light.

*

In Dumbo I walked around crying for no reason.

*

In this postcard, I tell her about the underwhelming fireworks. I tell her that Manhattan is a trite joke and not a *city*. I ask her for her definition of "city."
Then I extract my bad molar and attach it to the postcard. I slip the postcard+tooth in an envelope. I drop the envelope in a mailbox. I tongue the empty socket of my mailed molar.

*

The body is an *alien* intelligence.

*

When she sent me letters, she sent them doused in her perfume. The scent still lingers.

*

Her name, of course, was never Cleo. She admitted this when the knife was at my throat.

*

It had been raining.

*

We used to eat a special kind of sandwich. It had a special name. I remember the texture and constitution of this sandwich, *I can even taste it.* When my eyes are closed.

*

In Manhattan I developed an appreciation for gin and tonic. The colonial drink, from malarial lands. I sipped it at a rooftop bar.
Earlier, I had tried—and rejected—an old fashioned, a cosmopolitan, several kinds of martinis, I could not stand vermouth *stashed in lungs.* Grassy flavor. But gin and tonic—

*

I once fell in love with a rat. And the rat, in turn, fell in love with me.

*

The apartment was small but not unpleasant. On my first day, I bought a plastic plate, bowl, spoon, knife, fork, glass, mug, and an oscillating fan.
And several books, and a string of fairy lights.

*

I became sick in that room, a sickness that bored through the cone of vitality—I was reading, at that time, *The Black Dahlia*—but this was not until later, slightly later.

*

Café, roti with channa and potato. Ate many of these, lost count, while walking. Dirtying my shirt. Pleased.

*

In the park, there was a woman in red, dancing. She was on the grass by the lake and she had a boombox blasting samba, and she was dancing to it. People eddied around her. I stood behind a tree for a very long time, watching her, the sun set. She picked up her boombox and left.

*

Subway tracks.

*

Filthy whoosh of wind.

*

The *cosmic* wind! (But of course there is no *cosmos*)—only this river of shit.

*

Intimacy, I called it. Later, later. My friend, who heard me mumble the word, arched her eyebrow in irony.

*

Also sent her nail clippings. These parts of me are *holy,* I screamed into the postcard. So those pieces of me were shuttled through the postal system, and I felt the pain in my spine. Like a series of small kicks.

*

She liked the skin behind the knees.

*

Her arm as it wrapped around my neck. Collapsing space. There was music and the lights were low. Too much smoke tearing at my eyes. Her nails, leaving marks.

*

It was raining, 2 a.m.

*

This time I am sending her my hair. All of it.

*

Biker takes a curve too quick. Splinters of kneecap. I catch one in my fist.

*

I remember the roommate sometimes often, sweat as it collected at the base of her throat. That strange anatomical hollow. Designed maybe just for me.

*

The seasons have stopped shifting here. Now it's just—this, single, matte.

*

A flower that blooms into blood. I have cupped it in my gentle palm. Careful not to erupt. And she, as she opened her mouth and took the flower. Its bloody pap sank into her. Gliding down her esophagus, and then the other canals.

*

We were in Tribeca. And then we were not.

*

The length of history sleeps here. In these streets which burn with an acid smell.

*

Open your soft mouth. Tongue. Texture different from cow tongue, which I ate yesterday at a small café. Cow tongue, cow spleen, some sauces and a lettuce leaf, in a soft sesame bun.

*

Soft mouth. YOURS! I am dribbling into it.

*

Cow mouth.

*

Like letters. And she sent me nothing back. The universe, between us, folds on itself and gathers knots, entangled, I will take a pair of scissors to its folds. The universe sits between us like a fat cow.

*

The moments were short. Bursting like bone. She was here. And then not.

*

We were alone in the back room. She crooked her leg around me.

*

Outside, slouched against the wall, my friend was having a heart attack. When I found him he insisted it was nothing, but his red face, his abnormal breathing. We were in the ER, then, and a nurse escorting him away from me.

*

A pencil stuffed into the soft flesh behind the knees.

*

Later, I'll watch a movie with a friend. We'll go to a cinema, the one with only ten seats. It's a single room with a projector and a screen. We will watch a B-movie there, something horrible. With popcorn. With milkshakes or beer. Then I will go alone again. It will be just me, alone in there. And ghosts. Their presence so fleshy it's almost corporeal.

*

And Cleo. The tilt of her head. The way she smiled.

*

Cleo joins me in my postcards. We're at a café together, sipping coffee and preparing a postcard. I wrote this one in pink ink. Something in me—I have known this too long, denying it—has been dying, diseased. I'm on my way out. This might be the last postcard. I can't bear the thought of it. I cry all over the postcard, Cleo patting my shoulder. I enclose my eyelashes. Cleo plucked them for me. She eats one, for good luck she says. The rest I carefully situate in the envelope, along with the postcard and its smudges of pink. Overcome, I add my thumb to the packet. Cleo scolds me.

*

I continue to feel the presence of my thumb. I woke up sucking it this morning, sucking my absent thumb. Regressing.

*

Pineal gland. I tap it in its vase.

*

Nothing much happened in the Champagne Room. We talked and played a card game. Drank something. Cleo read my palm. She told me I had a frog in place of a heart. And that, for longevity, I should ingest six frog legs every day. Then Cleo fucked me for fun.

*

Listening to Michael Jackson while the car battery fades. Hoping the city will drown me somehow. Feeling all accreted like brain sand, something inconsequential like that.

*

Others' eyes. We must gouge these out with forks and knives.

*

Manhattan as infinite approach. In this sense like the asymptote. Which is constant striving, more and more futile as it grows. There, there. Which is nowhere.

*

The yellow cab from JFK.

*

Throttling down those filthy streets, insubstantial as air. I leak through the windows, vibrating into the night.

*

She pins me to the bed and smokes a cigarette.

*

I can feel a bedbug chewing on me.

*

A heart attack in the Hotel Dixie.

*

The stripper whose body was found under the bed, covered in plastic garbage bags. Body festering with burn marks, eaten by cockroaches.

*

Lizards peeking from the eye sockets.

*

A patina of lizard eggs over your skin, cracked and opening.

*

I caressed her soft face. We rubbed our cheeks together, fell asleep huddled like halfmoons.

*

In this dream, a woman is asphyxiating with her head in a bag. It's a plastic grocery bag, the groceries still in it. Onions, garlic, and tomatoes clatter around her bluing face.

*

Tilt your head down like a deer and drink.

*

She wrenched my jaw around. Straddled me.

*

Her tongue was in my mouth.

*

Someone played incoherent music.

*

Her tongue was in my mouth, then it was in my gut.

*

Her hand stroking the left side of my neck, pausing at the base of my throat. Sudden swell in the volume of my ghosts.

*

It's been years. Dreaming of Cleo. Pig city made a pig of me.

*

Standing by the mailbox. Waiting for an envelope.

IN CONVERSATION WITH VI KHI NAO

Ayirani Balachanthiran

VI KHI NAO: Your art exhibits a lot of ecosensuality and femininity and feels quite eco-serenic as well. Through your art, are you hoping to advocate for tenderness between women and nature? What kind of emotional landscape do you wish your viewers to experience when they are exposed to your work?

AYIRANI BALACHANTHIRAN: Can I ask what ecosensuality is? I haven't heard of the term before.

VKN: I guess a word I just invented to depict your work, where it embraces or marries ecology with sensuality?

AB: I like that a lot! I definitely want to link sensuality with my love for plants and just nature itself, but to go beyond the typical trope of "mother nature." More of an affirmation that women of color are natural and that we belong here—sort of as a response to growing up in a Western environment and being compared to white women? Typically, brown women aren't afforded the same softness or fragility. And I want to show we are soft and have deep feelings!

VKN: What is your favorite art piece of yours? And, could you describe why you love it? May I have an image of it?

AB: At the moment, my favorite piece is my "Sun" card from my lesbian tarot series. The sketch had been sitting around for a while and after a long time I suddenly had the inspiration and idea to add in certain elements. I feel warm just looking at the piece and feel like it radiates strength, love, and passion.

VKN: How do you define soft, Ira? I really love how tender you portray brown women. As if you understand the language of love and indirectly advocate for the nonexistent language of war.

AB: To me, "soft" is all the things I couldn't be growing up. I speak from experience and think many other women have felt they have to be strong and bear innumerable burdens. Because it's a cliché that womanhood is difficult and involves suffering in exchange for our blessings. I want other women to be able to be vulnerable and really put themselves first, because being "hard" or "strong" all the time is tiring. To be soft is to admit when you are tired or scared or need something, and to allow yourself to be helped. I think there's intense pressure for many Asian women to take care of their family even at the cost of their own mental/physical health.

VKN: I feel so at peace when I view your work. Like a transformative feeling of being accepted and wanted. How long did it take you to make that piece? These floral arrows traffick the landscape of intent with such rosy, verdant, serenic warmth. Have you thought about turning that white arrow into a yellow rose? If a rose is a significant symbol in your work, what does it symbolize for you?

AB: I had started the sketch months ago, in April? I did not look at it again until June, a little bit before NYC Pride. When I first made the sketch, I had the intent of embedding this piece with strength and vigor! But I was stuck on it for a little bit and ended up working on other pieces. When I returned to this one, I worked on it straight for like eight hours. I tend to make most of my art in large chunks of time because I focus best that way. I don't know the overall time spent, but I go back and readjust the colors and small things like a hundred times because I'm very picky. I chose to put roses in place of arrows to add a dreamy/ironic element. A regular archer releases arrows to inflict pain, but roses are associated with beauty, love, and elegance. She's [the sun] giving that to us. I love the idea of the arrow being a yellow rose! I had made all the roses closer to the arrow in full bloom with the ones farther away still budding. It would have been really great to have the main point of the piece be a yellow rose in full bloom . . . ! Roses are one of my favorite flowers, and I'm an idealist/dreamer with romance on my mind all the time, so it's important to my own personal aesthetics.

VKN: I love how some of your roses look like they have eyes, waiting to open. Others, they are wide open, but longing for their arrival. And, how some swim like fish, leaves as fins and mouth round like waiting to kiss or be kissed. If your rose arrows are not designed to inflict, what do you hope they inflict? And, where do you wish these roses to arrive at their final destination? After some time traveling through air, which could poison their vitality and liveliness.

AB: Yes! They have some motion and energy of their own. Swooping forward towards the center, the ones closest that are blooming are what I imagine we strive to be. To fully bloom, and we get there through a process; the ones behind will meet them at some point. They are here to bring admiration and affirmation to those who've needed it most! Especially for people who are not recognized for their beauty and worth. It's a recognition of true beauty, not the superficial construct our society capitalizes on. There aren't a lot of things that uplift and affirm queer women, and this piece is like my own love letter to everyone out there. Although most of my works are intended to express my own respect and love towards our community.

VKN: To build your own personal aesthetics, are there artists who have influenced your work? Or artists whom you admire?

AB: I don't really know any classical famous artists. I just follow other artists on Instagram and really enjoy their work. A few years ago I started really getting into Instagram and discovered a huge community of queer Asian artists and was so surprised. I didn't really know I was gay until I was eighteen or nineteen so I was kind of late to the big gay party. But it was so amazing to see their artworks and realize I could draw whatever I wanted. And then later on finding more and more people who share similar experiences and ideals about the world.

VKN: I was late to the gay party too. I still don't know how to party. Which Instagram artists do you follow? Do you wish to share a few you love? And, what do you love/admire about their work?

AB: I used to feel self-conscious about how late I acknowledged my sexuality. But I have learned to forgive myself because I wasn't in a welcoming environment and did my best to survive even if it meant repressing what I felt. I learned it doesn't really matter when but rather what you do, and how you build your queer family. Here are just a few of the many amazing people I follow on Instagram: @avant.guardianangel, @ch444n_, @em_niwa, @_mohtz, and @jasjyotjasjyot!

VKN: I am able to view a few of the amazing artists you follow: @em_niwa's work is somewhat like yours in the ecosensual sense. I am fond of how devilishly charming and comedic @ch444n_'s work is. In which direction do you foresee your work five or ten years from now? What kind of art do you wish to pursue down the road? Or is it a hard place for you to imagine?

AB: Em's work is really beautiful and I love their use of color so much. Their pieces are always full to the brim with flowers and luxury. Chawntell is super cool and I love the wild vibe of her pieces. Hmm, five or ten years is a long time, and personally I don't think that far ahead, but I hope by then I've mastered another medium and am making artwork that's totally different or more evolved! I feel like my art is constantly changing so much and that excites me.

VKN: Which medium do you imagine yourself mastering? And, what is your definition of mastery?

AB: I dabbled in oil painting for about a year or so, and thoroughly enjoyed it. But it was difficult for me to continue because at the time I was really depressed so even just the motions of cleaning up and setting up all the supplies and things needed was overwhelming. It's also kind of expensive, since you have to keep buying colors and canvas material. It wasn't sustainable for me at that time, but now I'm at a whole different level in my life and want to return to it! It's a wonderful medium and I enjoy how slowly it dries. It gives me so much time to bond with my painting and really think about what I want to add/change, etc. I hope in the future I'll be more financially stable and can oil paint to my heart's desire without worry of depleting supplies.

VKN: I hope that for you too, Ira! This may be non-sequitur since the question isn't about the fiscal affordability of oil paint, but when was the first time you fell in love, Ira? What was it like? Is there an art piece of yours that expresses this experience well or somewhat remotely closely?

AB: The first time I realized I was in love dawned on me long after it had already happened. I'm a bit slow to acknowledge my own feelings sometimes, but it was really innocent and pure. That feeling of just wanting to be around that person and be close to them. This oil painting had that essence.

VKN: Have you seen the 1996 Deepa Mehta film titled *Fire*? What did you think of it? Does it convey the emotional and aesthetic content of non-Westerned lesbian love you desire? Or does it fail? If it fails, how so? If it succeeds—in what way did it succeed? And, what is the best lesbian film and art piece you have ever encountered? What made it the best for you?

AB: I have! It was actually a bit triggering at first to watch, but I continued because it was like nothing I had ever seen before. I could really feel their tension and attraction. It was almost surreal to see people who looked like me onscreen, expressing desires we can't even imagine surfacing within our communities. It's so painful to have your deepest passions bubbling deep down and know that they could jeopardize your life. Though it wasn't their choice to be exposed, their decision to leave and choose a life for themselves in the end really inspired me, and gave me hope for my own future.

VKN: Is your family accepting of your lesbianism? Have you come out to both of your parents? Are you close to your mother/father?

AB: My parents are conservative Hindus, so they are extremely opposed to my sexuality. I was never close to either of my parents my entire life; we have always been at a distance. A distant family member had found an article that interviewed me about my art and sent it to my parents. I never came out to them, but this is how they found out. They immediately confronted me when I came home from work that day, and after that my life got considerably worse. I had cut my hair short a while before that, so my parents were already quite upset with me for going against the grain, but this was it. They made it impossible to live at home, so I saved up for a year and just recently moved out. I feel like I've finally escaped and am starting my life! Now I'm free to make art and be as gay as I want! I've lost the rest of my family, but I still keep in touch with my sisters only. I love them!

VKN: I am sorry to hear that, Ira, but it is also so amazing and fearless of you to be able to leave. I congratulate you on crossing such an extraordinary obstacle. I can imagine how transformative this departure is for you and how terrifying too! What are your sisters like, Ira?

AB: Thank you! It took a whole year of really hustling to save up and lots of therapy sessions, but I finally gained the confidence to find a new job and move out! Leaving was really scary and I had to deal with screaming and conflict, but I made it! I acknowledge I had many privileges that other queer people who have had to leave their homes didn't have. I have two sisters, one older and one younger. We have really large age gaps, so growing up we weren't very close, but in recent years we've become really tight. I'm closer with my little sister because I did a lot of parenting; I had to do things for her that my parents were unable to provide. I spoil her a bit, but my biggest goal is to give her everything I didn't have, and make sure she doesn't make the same mistakes as me. My big sister is an Aquarius so it's kind of hard to talk to her. But she is well-meaning and knowledgeable. She suffered so much, and I respect her and appreciate the advice she gives me.

VKN: What sign are you?

AB: I'm a Libra! Always dreamy.

VKN: And, which sign do you along most or most compatible with?

AB: My best friend is a Sagittarius and I also know a ton of Libras, weirdly. I love other Libras the most!

VKN: If a dish (foodwise) could be ecosensual, which dish would that be?

AB: There are these Korean bakeries that have clear jelly cakes, or some kind of dessert that has flowers in it. Like actual petals and edible gold foil; it's all very beautiful. I love how pretty they are but haven't tried them myself.

VKN: What is the composition of your race/ethnicity, Ira? Have others confused you for a different race or ethnicity?

AB: I am Sri Lankan Tamil, raised in New York. I have actually been taken for many different races; I've been asked if I was Spanish, Middle Eastern, etc. by people at work or in school. I guess I have a racially ambiguous face. But I've also encountered many brown people are who shocked that I am brown because it's kind of rare for brown women to dress/act this way, I guess.

VKN: How is your day today, Ira? What did you do? Do you usually eat late or early? And, are you reading anything wonderful? Or music-wise, listening to anything worth noting?

AB: It was good! It had some ups and down. I went to work and was excited all day to go to this lesbian book club thing my friend told me about, but I didn't realize until after that I missed the signup sheet so I was disappointed! But I ended up hanging out with my friend anyway and we had fun, so overall it was a good day! I always eat toast with butter in the morning; it's my favorite thing ever to eat, super easy food especially if you're too depressed/tired to cook or do anything. My best friend works at a bookstore and always gives me books, and I recently got *Mostly White* by Alison Hart—about the experiences of Native American boarding schools. It's a heartbreaking read, but I'm also full of rage that we never learned about this in school and want to know their story. I am currently enjoying Blood Orange's latest album, and also "Hold On" by The Internet—SO soft and dreamy!

VKN: Are you a fan of the Kardashians? If one of them asked you to paint them, which one would you most likely paint? And, of your five toes, which toe do you feel most close to? Painting-wise. Nail painting, I meant.

AB: That's not a question I expected! I really dislike all that they stand for but appreciate the memes made about their antics. I would totally do that for money. If I had to, I guess I would paint Kourtney; she's kind of underrated. I like my big toe because it's the easiest to paint!

VKN: With all of that money, you could make more oil paintings? Is there a Sri Lankan Tamil artist, writer, or poet that you read, admire, or desire to emulate?

AB: I could totally make more oil paintings! But I might buy some more house plants first. I can't think of a Sri Lankan Tamil artist specifically, but my friend Anju is an Indian-Tamil artist. She dabbles in different art mediums like poetry, photography, curating, etc., and is one of my biggest inspirations. We became friends through Instagram. I had followed her work and bought one of her poetry books. I forgot how we started talking but she came to visit NYC and I got to show her around to some cool places. The first time I saw her I almost dropped my phone because of how pretty she is! Her art and experiences resonate with me so much. We have only hung out in person a few times but even just that first time I felt like I had known her for so long. All of her work has the same luxurious essence, and I aspire to have that in my art as well.

VKN: Which house plants do you have in mind? Anju seems like such an exquisite artist! Time to date her? How shy do you feel about being assertive about your desire?

AB: I really want a Pilea (aka Chinese money plant). I'm going to collect all the different money plants there are. I find it hilarious every culture has a different plant they call a money plant, so I think if I get them all I'll be rich one day! Or at least happy with such a variety of plants to keep me company. Anju is my muse, and I admit many of the women in my artworks have her resemblance. She knows this and I also have a portrait of her in oil that I need to finish! As much as I admire her, I haven't really thought about anything more—she lives so far! Maybe one day! I am usually pretty upfront with flirting and have no issues with telling people how I feel.

VKN: Money plant! I love that! I am happy and admire that you are so brave about being canonical with your attraction. That's too bad she is so far away.

AB: Right? So fun! I think fate will bring us together again at some point, even if it's just briefly. I look forward to it!

NIGHTSTAND

Encina Roh

the humming of the refrigerator hollows out
the space between the last of your words
that have been absorbed by the bedroom.
   unkindly preserved between the mirror and electric currents,
   you are a creature paled and washed down
   by the dense velvet of rain clouds and small traumas.
your last guest is lemon rind,
bitter and fragrant,
a thing you cannot stomach
unless she is diluted with sugar and butter.
   you pause before closing the door,
   familiarizing yourself with the equipoise of your own
   presence again and conclude that letting others
   leave with your loneliness in their purse is theft.
a siren wails in the distant streets of the city
(she would wonder whether it is rushing to or from disaster)
but you mourn all the same.

ADULTERY I

Encina Roh

at dusk,
untuck me from your cellar
and core me with the unripe fruit in your sink.

    my skin is maroon wax
    like chrysanthemum petals
    unfurling rhythmically from the space between
    your copper thumb and the knife.

half of me is in your hand,
seedless gut exposed,
as you tell her
there are leftovers in the fridge
for tomorrow.

ADULTERY II

Encina Roh

hunger dissolves the butterflies
in my stomach and my tongue
curls over the soft wings and waxy bodies
of their little corpses.
i chew what has been swallowed,
i have eaten worse than this.

11:59

Encina Roh

new year's eve next year,
the clock is reset and the night is still.

a hundred thousand boxes of light
stare at you and you feel alone and watched at the same time.

the silhouettes tenting over dinners and television sets
are characters in fiction and isolation
gathers around you like paper confetti.

you let insignificance dissolve on your tongue,
turning the crackers and pomegranate soda
into a bitter paste.

REAPING

Encina Roh

heal me with
the September equinox,
where blue workers
gather their crop and seed
and Autumn faintly
reminds painted leaves
and swollen elderberries
to script
the epilogue of
inflorescence
and ripened memories.

PEACE

Encina Roh

to fall asleep, you
coerce her existence into unfinished lines
and hang her with your midnight laundry

you cannot breathe against her vices
and you know well enough that there
will never be a contradiction in misery

under stale linen
you remind yourself each evening
that daybreak exists only a few hours away.

she tells you to dress for god
and you reply that god has no eyes

THE TIGER SLEEPS AT DAWN

artemis lin

My mother calls the tattooed woman *yě*.
   In Mandarin, a word that holds all forms of *wild*;
      "a wild woman," i.e. a woman no holds barred, a woman

untamed. She seeks to tame me in the word.
   Stakes me to the floor with her gaze. I remember
      my art history professor telling me, we Chinese,

we have a strange relationship with nature. We revere
   its old wisdom, yet seek to tame it. Lay down long odes
      to the noble pine, and in same breaths clear forests.

Holding both to be true. My mother watches and seeks my gaze.
   I wanted a tattoo once, actually. Telling me who I can
      or cannot be. Telling me not to be feral, not

to eat, teeth bared. Can't show my hunger or my empty *hunger*.
   I wanted the tattoos on my wrists, as lassos, or how
      a tugboat might lead the largest vessel back from

the sea. Virginia Woolf drowned herself, you know. And she was
   wild. Wildest woman I knew. She knows my face. Like the tallest
      pine, reaching, I do find solace in the sun. The sun so bright

I can barely see.

PITH

Sydney S. Kim

She presses her thumb into the top of the orange. As she looses peel from flesh, the whole world turns.

Mother ate so many clementines her palms turned orange. This is a story that is told over and over, as though the act of consuming alone was worthy of boasting. Hunger does not factor.

They never really ate dessert after dinner; only fruit. Blade to peel, skin coming off in one long spiral. Careful hands pick stringy white pith from precious fruit. Jeweled pulp encased in semi-opaque membrane—each slice is a womb.

The orange always comes back up at night. Undigested pith, pulp mash, acid that leaves the throat burning. Even so, the sting is sugared.

She's never had to free her food from its trappings. Crab claws cracked open by others, sweet white meat piled on a plate, just for her. Thin armor peeled from shrimp in C-shaped shells. All she has to do is grasp it by its tail. The abundance renders her helpless. Her hands are soft and pale and decidedly plain.

The first time she makes herself bleed, she feels a sense of pride. All on her own, she has managed to breach the epidermis. The red is nectar and a promise of something more. If only she could go deeper, she could reveal whatever essence she thinks she's been missing all this time. But the pith is too thick, too soft, too white and her fingers are clumsy in their eagerness.

The first time she sees the girl, she imagines clinging to her skin like juice. Her presence a scent that won't wash off, lingering as a reminder each time the girl touches her face. The residue that coats her fingers when they come together is curious. It is enough until it isn't.

Questions layer over them like bitterness, useless cushion that separates her from something that she knows will taste sweeter.

Maybe the girl will allow her to pry, to continue her explorations into what they've made together. The girl doesn't, but she punctures the surface anyway. The hard crescent of her fingernail presses neatly into skin until it gives way and the scent of release fills the air. No truth goes unturned. Every question and every answer turns sour with each repetition.

Alone, she eats until it's all run dry. The orange always comes back up.

PRISM 1

PRISM 2

PRISM 3

PRISM 4

IN CONVERSATION WITH VI KHI NAO

Sydney S. Kim

VI KHI NAO: Your work is genre-crossing, moving in various mediums. Which medium do you feel least at home in? Meaning, if your art is kinetic, what aspect of it invites the most resistance? And, when is it a good time to embrace opposition in one's work?

SYDNEY S. KIM: This is something I'm still figuring out. The answer changes every few years or so. I used to feel very close to drawing, but lately, not so much. My visual work tends to be driven by intuition, instinct . . . it took me some time to learn how to home in on what was working and not working about my process and compositions. I learned the rhythms of drawing and mark-making, learned how to focus so I wasn't going in blind every time I sat down with paper and pencil. I've spent some time away from drawing, so the process feels a bit opaque to me right now—which is frustrating, but also freeing. Because there isn't outside pressure forcing me to reach any conclusions about my compositions, however, I'm able to experiment more without worrying where my hand is taking me. I'm open to seeing where it goes.

VKN: I noticed there is great tenderness in both your visual and written work. Are tenderness and the unknown important aspects of your work? Do you feel that one is able to access tenderness more with drawings or with writing? Or do you feel that they are interchangeable?

SSK: I think intimacy is an important aspect of my work. I've heard that my visual work feels intimate, but I'm not sure if it's because of the trappings of the particular color palette I'm drawn to, or the delicacy of the marks and textures I favor. The experience is different, I think, when one is looking at a piece of artwork or reading a piece of writing. Unless the artwork is very figurative, one's reaction tends to be more abstract and thus potentially harder to place. It can be more direct with writing due to the inherent nature of language, whether read or heard. They both have immense staying power, but I feel like the flavor is different. When it comes to creating, the experience is very different for me. Drawing can feel more cathartic because it's so physical, almost like a direct line to the feeling. Writing can be trickier and is less immediate because I take more time deliberating which word would make the best vessel for whatever it is I'm trying to convey.

VKN: I think your literary products are also intimate and I know you're drawn to fantasy, at least from a literary standpoint. Do you foresee your drawings being moved to mimic intimately the literary form? Or do you feel different textural and philosophical impulses with each medium? And, what it is about the realm of the fantasy that catches your fancy?

SSK: I don't think so. At least for now. My visual work tends to be self-reflexive (with photography) . . . though, now that I'm thinking about drawing, I may be wrong. For a time, I was really digging deep into trauma and channeling psychic pain through my drawings. I've definitely explored some of those themes with my writing. My most recent drawings are formal experiments that explore the boundaries of shape and form, color and space. Possibly, this overlaps with my literary interest in genre-blurring!

My literary impulses are very idea-driven. I like to start with a seed—an image, a concept, a phrase—and spin a story around it, let it crystallize. It's a lot less concrete with my visual work.

Fantasy is very alluring to me. I love the possibility of new worlds, of mysterious systems that determine and drive characters' paths . . . It's a realm where I can really flex my imagination. I also love tradition, history, and ritual. Even if I'm drawing from examples that exist real world, I enjoy giving more power to those things in my fantasy pieces.

VKN: Are there limits to what fantasy can do? If so, what kind of limitations can they impose on your creative soul?

SSK: I have trouble with perfecting self-created systems. In the same way that science fiction still requires believable and working science (not always, but often), the systems and structures within fantasy still need to make sense. Sometimes I'll start with some sort of magic, ritual, location . . . but experience difficulty making it fully believable to the reader and, more importantly, real for the characters. In short, worldbuilding can be hard.

VKN: You write understated Asian sapphic eroticism with such confidence, creativity, and quiet assertiveness. Where do you draw this source of credence? My exposure to sapphic writing is limited and I have had little exposure to this community. Are there Asian queer role models in art and literature you turn to for inspiration? If so, who are they? And, what do you love most about their work? If not, are you working quietly in the dark like me too?

SSK: Thank you! I didn't really start thinking too deeply about the specific experience of being queer and Asian until more recently, sadly. Weirdly, the Asian part to that equation came later. It was gradual—grappling with that part of my identity and how it separated my own experience and narrative from other (non-Asian) queers I knew. I also didn't meet many queer people of color until adulthood, long after I came out (my college was pretty homogenous). It can be lonely.

I love Qiu Miaojin and I also love comic artists and illustrators like Mariko Tamaki and Takako Shimura. Other than that, I'm also in the dark. I'm drawn to the rawness of Qiu Miaojin's work. *Skim* by Jillian and Mariko Tamaki really captures the particular loneliness that can come with being young, Asian, and queer. I come back to that graphic novel a lot. *Aoi Hana* is a manga set in high school, which could potentially be tropey and cheesy but works because of how intimate and soft Takako Shimura draws and writes her characters—hands and fingers, soft yearning sentiments.

VKN: I am not familiar with the Tamakis' work and I look forward to exploring it in depth. Thank you for telling me about this. Speaking of graphics and moving graphics such as cinema, are there Asian films (not necessarily queer films) that speak in a language that queerly suspends one's relationship to loneliness? Have you seen the 2016 *Our Love Story* (Hangul: 연애담; RR: Yeon-ae-dam)? It's a South Korean lesbian film written and directed by Lee Hyun-ju, starring Lee Sang-hee and Ryu Sun-young. I thought the film captures more accurately some of the concerns (dutiful desire vs. dutiful obligation/obedience) Asian lesbians face in the modern world. Also, the love scenes were comedically tender and possibly defied expectations of eroticism.

SSK: Wong Kar-wai's *Happy Together*, for sure. Well, no, that's the opposite, actually. I think it exacerbates feelings of loneliness, but regardless, it's very moving and relatable. *Revolutionary Girl Utena* is also great. It's an animated film that's saturated with surreal, colorful imagery. The first time I saw it, I couldn't wrap my head around it (I was in high school and not out). The second time, everything clicked into place—high schoolers whose pastel-colored hair change lengths whenever their true selves awaken (on a dance floor or sword-fighting arena). It's all very coded and honestly quite bizarre, but ultimately, the movie is all about escaping societal oppression and celebrating queerness.

I've not seen [*Our Love Story*]! I will have to. I think part of me is sometimes scared to watch Korean films and television because of how real and close to home it all will feel. I remember watching *A Tale of Two Sisters* and crying at the end because I couldn't stop thinking about my family—specifically, my mother.

VKN: Your mother? What was the source of your tears?

SSK: Hilariously, I hesitate to go into too much detail because my mother prefers that I not talk about her family and family history. I'm not sure she will read this, though, so I'll go ahead. She had a difficult childhood and acted as the mother figure for her younger sisters. I'm not sure how familiar you are with the film, but it's centered around two sisters, their recently deceased mother, their absent father, and the new stepmother who has invaded the family home. It's really about how pride can conflict with the love we have for our immediate family. It's complicated. I saw my own mother in the older sister, her protectiveness. Tragic familial love—I don't think I'd ever seen that in a movie before.

VKN: I am not familiar with the film and I believe this interview is less likely to be published in a digitalized form as it's designed for print format, but one never knows. If you feel too raw with your reply, we can omit this question during the editing process. I am, however, curious and would love to know regardless of its omission potentiality.

SSK: That's okay! There's just this bit of intergenerational gap between immigrant parents and first-generation children. Sometimes, that gap gets closed very quickly and very intensely and suddenly, both sides see each other more clearly. I don't know if that makes sense.

VKN: Yes, it does make sense. I understand. Do you desire visibility for your sapphic material? Or do you prefer some opacity as opacity can provide space and enclosure to work out the neophytal queer kinks in one's work before it is brought out into light?

SSK: I definitely desire visibility for my queer materials. If only to connect with more Asian queer women. And overall, I just want my work to connect with people. I'll always be private when it comes to the act of making. I also feel that the ways in which I explore and express queer identity will always be somewhat shrouded or abstracted. I'm interested in pain and the failures of intimacy as well, so I'm a little worried people might think my work is too dark.

VKN: I do not think your work is dark. It goes into known places and I suppose others may view such intimate uncertainty as dark, but for me, more paradoxically, your work has a levity to it. A work that speaks more about levitation and suspension like how modern bridges function in this world. These levitational bridges in your work provide concrete passages from one plane of reality to the next. What is your ideal creative invention? What is the shape and gaze of that potential invention? What kind of viewership/readership do you seek? Do you have a long-term vision or goal for your work? What is the best way to respond to your future productivity?

SSK: Thank you. I have a couple of book ideas mapped out. I have a novella nearly fully outlined, as well as a novel. There are also two short stories I've written—one of which you've read, "The Haenyeo's Daughter"—set in the same world, and those could potentially turn into a novel. Though each of these projects is very different, they all contain that soft fantasy element. I'd like to reach queer people of color who enjoy both literary and genre fiction. Genre can be tough; the trappings and formulas of fantasy and science fiction can be very seductive, and though I think a lot of writers are doing great work with pushing the boundaries of what it can offer, readers can be resistant. The same can be said for the literary realism audience. The two can coexist, though, and I'd like people to be open to work that occupies that liminal space. That's what I'm trying to do, at least, as a writer.

VKN: How long does it take you to write literary pieces like "The Haenyeo's Daughter"? And, what event (if any) in your life sets the story in literary motion for you?

SSK: It really depends. That story took me about a few days to write. Then maybe a week of revisions. Other stories have taken me a lot longer. Months. The outlining process takes the bulk of my time. Once I've worked everything out—solidified each little node—then I finally start writing. What do you mean with the last question? Like what inspires/sparks it?

VKN: Yes, exactly. What sparks it? Have you been to Iceland before? Your work reminds me of the entire continent of Nordic glacier and Iceland. The crystallization of time and the subliminal milieu—geysers and the lava-like nature of your characters and the strong elemental quality of arctic electricity; the distance it takes for one woman (being) to be close to another woman (being)—in your stories give me the impression that your writing and our time on earth can be crystallized into pockets of intergalactic memory, potentially extraterrestrial parable, and nomadic intimacy.

SSK: It depends! Sometimes an image will materialize and wedge itself into my head. Other times, I'll be fixated on a particular concept, which will then branch out and grow like a rhizome.

I have! It was incredible. I went with my girlfriend in late November two years ago. I chose winter dates on purpose. I wanted an extreme experience. It was beautiful. Transcendent. I'd been wanting to visit Iceland since college—Roni Horn was one of my favorite artists and she's done a lot of work about that magical place.

Iceland is potent with metaphor, as you pointed out. I'm rather preoccupied with memory and landscape and the weather there is everchanging, which means the land around you is also always in flux. We drove all around the coast in different types of weather—rain, dawn fog, clear noon, pitch-black night—cliffs and grass and lava and waterfalls came in and out of view, changed color. It felt new every minute. Which meant that it was sort of inherently difficult to commit to memory.

It also did really feel like we were on a different planet. I know everyone talks about the black lava sand and basalt, but what struck me the most was the grass and moss. Sometimes the light was pink and the grass, orange. Other times, it was golden and painterly. Very strange. I imagine the deserts out here seem alien to Icelandic visitors.

VKN: It sounds absolutely marvelous. Did your story attempt to capture this beautiful experience?

SSK: Actually, no. I resisted the urge to represent! I actually remember at one point we were driving, and I said out loud to Jenevive, "What's the point of painting when all of this exists? Why would anyone even try?" I think trying to make art about Iceland is a bit futile, haha.

VKN: Do you wish to respond to (not capture) this arctic-like landscape with your visual art/drawings?

SSK: Yes, but maybe not in an obvious way. I'm really interested in this idea that nothing is static. The black sand beaches had some areas that were taped off. It was too dangerous and the sea, too violent and unpredictable. Like, truly sudden—people can literally get swept away in the blink of an eye. Same with the glaciers. Unless you're a professional tour guide, you're not supposed to walk on them on your own because the ice is shifting and moving all the while. If you venture out on your own, you probably won't be able to find your way back. I like that. The idea of an autonomous and occasionally hostile environment.

VKN: Speaking of ice shifting, is your sexual orientation like such black sand beaches and the inconsistent surface of glacier? Are you bi or are you drawn predominantly to women? When did you know?

SSK: I'm definitely drawn more towards women. I'll find a man attractive every once in a blue moon, but it doesn't mean anything. My coming out experience wasn't very typical. I didn't even consider it a possibility for the longest time. When a friend jokingly suggested it, a light just turned on in my head, like, "oh." Then in college, I got the chance to explore it and it became real. I was very private about it for a while. Consumed a lot of bad gay movies and lesbian pulp fiction in my messy dorm room while I was severely depressed. Then I spent a summer in New York and got to really explore it. Went to all the lesbian dance clubs and bars. Danced and made out with girls. Got a really terrible haircut. It was a time.

VKN: Ah, latent desire manifested into lifestyle. How do you like your coffee? Do you drink coffee? And, is there an Asian dish you could not live without?

SSK: I do! I drink it black. I make pour over coffee every morning. I like cold brew, too. I prefer the Ethiopian varieties. I could not live without my mom's kimchi chigae. I'm also crazy for kalguksu! I don't know, now that I live in LA, even though I can eat all the Asian food I want, I want even more. I love it all.

VKN: I love Asian dishes too. I can't live without white rice. Why the Ethiopian varieties?

SSK: They're fruity and floral! Very flavorful. I like fruity things. Pinot noir is my favorite wine.

VKN: Will you tell me about your love story of your girlfriend? How did you meet? And, how do you define the nature of falling in love? What is your definition of falling? Do you have great balance? Are you good at walking on a moving train?

SSK: Oh my gosh. We actually met through missed connections on Craigslist, if you can believe it.

I don't know. I've only been in love twice. Both times, I saw it coming. I don't know how. I just felt it. I have okay balance. I'm good at walking on a moving train if the train is a familiar one.

VKN: Oh, my goodness! Craigslist! The place where one sells iPods? And, bookshelves and awkward furniture?

SSK: Haha, yes! Do you know about missed connections?

VKN: How sci-fi of you! I may have heard of them, but not really. Perhaps you can educate me.

SSK: Okay, so it's a page where people can post ads about strangers they saw or bumped into. Felt an attraction to. If you brush shoulders with someone on the G train and you locked eyes. But then the subway doors closed, and she was gone. That sort of thing. You describe the person you saw, you describe yourself, and then the moment. Anyway, I saw her at a house party, but I'd actually seen her twice around town before (we were in Portland, Oregon at the time). The third time I decided to approach her. She was unreceptive. I went home and drunkenly posted an ad on missed connections. A week later, she responded! Hilariously, when I'd met her at the party, I was with my friend, Mimi, who is also Asian. We were also both wearing light blue shirts . . . I had described myself as being Asian and wearing a light blue shirt. Oops. Our correspondence tapered off, but then I saw her at an art event and mustered up the courage to talk to her. She was very awkward, but we ended up making plans for coffee.

VKN: Like this YouTube video? https://www.youtube.com/watch?v=63CE6AfD7YE

SSK: Oh my god, I've seen that! I saw it on Logo, hahaha.

#INMEMORIAM

Tessa Yang

In Lila's last profile picture, she crouches on the sidewalk in paint-spattered jeans, one foot raised above a graffitied fire hydrant, lips drawn back in what is either cheesy grin or snarl.

Lila's last cover photo: a still from an obscure French film. Half-naked women in a bathhouse drape themselves over lounge chairs like so many towels, wilted from heat.

Lila's last Facebook status bemoans the ills of Facebook, though she monitored her likes obsessively and combed her newsfeed for gossipy tidbits eight times a day.

The last person she friended was named Philip Baker-Horowitz, a soccer player with a receding hairline and an acne-pocked forehead. He did not, as far as I know, attend the funeral.

The last photo Lila posted was of her dinner Tuesday night—sushi, which she ordered and ate in obscene quantities, even in our landlocked college town nine hundred miles from the nearest ocean where all seafood was suspect.

The last photo she was tagged in came from the improv team's page. *LILA PARK LEADS A TEAM OF EAGER FIRST-YEARS IN AN ICEBREAKER ACTIVITY AT ORIENTATION.* The first-years don't look so eager, but Lila does.

The last timeline Lila posted on was mine, though I wouldn't see it till six days after the funeral when I returned to Facebook feeling raw, dried-out—some dehydrated fruit version of me. There were messages from dozens of relatives and friends who were thinking about me, praying for me, now that Lila was gone. She didn't include a relationship status on her profile, but everyone knew what we were to each other.

I'm an anomaly for my generation. A technophobe among legions of savvy millennials with punny Twitter handles and carefully calibrated Instagram aesthetics. I can go weeks without checking my Facebook. My profile picture remains that generic person-shaped cutout on a light blue background. Lila used to make fun of me for this.

What she posted on my timeline was a Buzzfeed article about two Asian grannies recently arrested outside Memphis for a shoplifting spree: $12,000 worth of tech gadgets, jewelry, and rare LEGO sets lifted from various malls and stored in their garage over a period of fifteen months. It was the perfect con. Who would suspect two cheery old crones pushing covered strollers where surely grandchildren lay sleeping? Who would notice them at all?

In their mug shots, one woman bares a set of gleaming dentures; the other grimaces, unimpressed, a huge sty on her left eyelid like a fleshy pom-pom.

What are your retirement plans? Lila posted beneath the article. *#goals.*

THOU SHALT RIDE ALL THE DINOSAURS

Tessa Yang

The craft project on the first day of Vacation Bible School is a construction paper dinosaur. Naturally, this inspires a number of urgent questions.

Who would win in a fight: A T. rex or a Transformer?

Did the dinosaurs come before God, or after?

If I found a dinosaur egg, would I raise it as my own or give it to the police?

"T. rex," I say. "After. Raise it as my own." I vary my responses depending on my mood and who's asking. Shy Tasha who taps my lower back when she wants something. Freckly Seth, who achieved pariah status the first five minutes of camp for accidentally calling me "Mom." Lucas, the troublemaker, who pasted fourteen googly eyes on the stomach of his triceratops and begins sprinting ahead of the class as soon as we leave the school building.

"Buddy system, Lucas!" Mai warns, and he halts at the edge of the parking lot, arms windmilling, paper dinosaur flapping in the breeze.

Latched at the hands, we cross the parking lot as one, a small mob of preschoolers and two sweaty women in bright yellow T-shirts. I joked with Mai at orientation that our color assignment was racially motivated, so they could identify us from a distance. Mai smiled and said, "Speak for yourself. I look great in yellow." And she does. She looks great in every color.

Inside the gym, two middle-aged women dispense paper cups full of rainbow Goldfish, juice boxes, and napkins patterned with tiny dinosaurs that all the children but Tasha will ignore, preferring to wipe their sticky mouths on knuckles and sleeves. The theme of this year's Vacation Bible School is "Let the earth bring forth living creatures," but I suspect the dinosaur angle arises from the recent release of Chris Pratt's *Jurassic World*—an efficient, if slightly desperate marriage between scripture and pop culture that makes me smile.

Mai shouts for everyone to come together so we can say a prayer. She's a serial prayer. In the car, before bed, when thunder shudders through the walls of our apartment and when the sun emerges after, filling the yard with steam. She prays cheerfully, as if she's reaching out to an old buddy with no particular agenda. *Hey, Jesus, it's Mai, just checking in.* Me, I pray like some underemployed toady desperate for a raise, brown-nosing, making promises I can't keep.

The kids bow their heads and clasp their fingers. Even Lucas speaks this language better than me. Mai makes a quick, comfortable utterance. Then Goldfish are crammed between lips and the children, freshly energized, challenge one another to perform their very best dinosaur impressions.

Over T. rex roars and pterodactyl shrieks, Seth asks whether Adam and Eve were allowed to ride the dinosaurs.

"Of course," I tell him. "There's that line in Exodus: *Thou shalt ride all the dinosaurs.*"

He collapses into a fit of giggles. He knows he's being lied to, and he loves it.

Mai regards me reproachfully as Seth gallops away. "You know you really shouldn't make stuff up about the Bible. They'll go home and repeat it to their parents." But her lips are twitching, and I know she thought it was funny, too.

"Why not?" I protest. "Thou Shalt Ride All the Dinosaurs is at least as believable as Thou Shalt Not Bake the Gay Cakes, and there are a million people who think *that's* in there."

"We don't have to do this," says Mai. "I thought it could be fun. You love kids . . ."

"And they love me. I'm very popular."

"You are." She bumps my shoulder with her shoulder. We're surrounded by screaming children and other pairs of teachers sipping their juice boxes on the gym floor, but Mai's always had a way of making me feel like it's just the two of us, the first humans on a sunbaked plateau.

The truth is I don't know what we're doing here. I suspect my sustained half-belief in God doesn't count for much in this crowd, and Mai's habitual praying can't erase the fact that she views the Catholic Church itself as an obsolete machine. Maybe it's the novelty of the situation. Vacation Bible School is a secret from my family, who left the Church years before it was fashionable to do so, and from Mai's, who pray for her every week. There are faiths that are kinder to people like us, but before we leave—if we leave—we're trying this thing out together, safely camouflaged as sisters. Best friends.

I collect the stray paper cups that haven't made it to the garbage can while Mai gathers the kids. After a quick headcount, I take Seth's hand, and together we lead the way to music class, Mai bringing up the rear.

Tasha prods my tailbone. She and Harper have been having a heated discussion. They know *where* heaven is—10,000 feet above the moon, duh!—but they want to know *when*.

"Twenty seconds," I say.

Seth laughs again, clinging to my hand and gazing up at me with love in his eyes.

IN CONVERSATION WITH VI KHI NAO

Tessa Yang

VI KHI NAO: Can you talk a little about the inspiration behind your piece "#InMemoriam"? Although it is fiction, it reads very non-fictiony (if there is such a word). I even tried to google "Buzzfeed" and "Asian grannies" and "12K" and came up with nothing. I wasn't too disappointed, though. I love the repetition of "The last" as a way to open sentences. I frequently notice this gesture, in particular, in poetry. Do you feel that your work has poetic impulses? Or does it feel more flashy, as in borrowing rhetorical devices from flash fiction?

TESSA YANG: You know, I swear there was an article somewhere about these old lady shoplifters who were stealing expensive LEGO sets. But it's been years since I read it, so I couldn't tell you where it was from! I also know I read something at some point about a young person who had passed away, and his Facebook account became a kind of living memorial where people could share their memories of him. (This is apparently called a "Memorialized Account.") I found this idea to be at once very beautiful and very eerie, to think that your Facebook could just keep going after you were gone. Anyway, this is typically how inspiration works for me: a couple of ideas marinating in my head for a few months or years, and then finally they coalesce into a story.

I read a lot more poetry now than I used to, and I think (I hope!) my work has "poetic impulses." The shorter the piece, the more lyrical the sentences tend to be.

VKN: Do you feel "#InMemoriam" is lyrical?

TY: Not relative to some other flash fictions I've written, which could potentially pass for prose poetry among certain readers. But I think, as you've observed, the refrain carries some poem-like music. And of course, I compulsively read all my drafts out loud many, many times to try and find that perfect-sounding sentence or phrase.

VKN: In one of your bios, it stated that you are working on a novel. Can you talk a little about the novel you are working on? If you were to describe your work to a dinosaur (say a T. rex, then), how would you go about it? And, would you say it's more realistic (in the realm of realism) or more fantastic? Since you are a fan of Carmen Maria Machado's work, may I be oppositional and ask you which current living writer doesn't speak to your heart?

TY: The novel that I'm working on is a coming-of-age story that explores the boundary between reality and fantasy, between what's actually happening in a small town and what narratives people are telling themselves to serve their own interests. The narrator is an adolescent girl, mixed-race, spending the summer getting to know her father's side of the family after having been semi-estranged from him for most of her childhood. Basically, she gets caught up in a lot of drama, and really has to sort out for the first time in her life what she believes, and why. I would say it's a realist novel with the occasional foray into fantasy. I think a T. rex would be totally sold on this story, honestly. A T. rex knows all about what it's like to occupy that space between fact and fiction.

In general, if I don't love one book by an author, I don't go seeking more of their work; that makes it tough for me to say whether it's the writer who's not speaking to my heart, or whether it was something in the particular work. Anyway, I'm a little ashamed to say this is what happened when I read *Sputnik Sweetheart* by Haruki Murakami in grad school. The book really baffled me, and I didn't connect with it. I can't even remember it that well, which isn't usually a good sign. I'm quite determined to give his work another try, but I have so many friends who just love Murakami, and I can't say that his writing has resonated with me yet.

VKN: Perhaps you could give his *After the Quake: Stories* a try? I really enjoyed the stories in there. But then I read him a decade or so ago . . . However, I am excited for you to give birth to that novel completely! On a more comedic note, there is a subtle undercurrent of humor and comedic intelligence in both of your pieces. Is your relationship to comedy strong? Do you intentionally try to find wit in concealed places? Or does the accident of humor arrive because two thoughts collide at a speed you did not expect?

TY: Oh, I love "the accident of humor." That feels true to the way I think and write. I definitely don't approach a scene thinking, "This needs a joke right here." Humor is just organic to the way I understand the world. In fiction, the more emotionally charged the scene or scenario, the more I find myself leaning into levity. It offers some breathing room for me as a writer, while also intensifying the heavier emotional content by force of contrast. I think most readers appreciate a little humor, too, as long as the author isn't coming across as overly clever.

VKN: Both pieces you submitted appeared very tightly edited. Can you talk a little about your editing process? Do you write lots and then chisel down until there is nothing but a thumb of wood? Or are you a writer who adds things in painfully slowly, like watching a stroller crossing a street without wheels?

TY: I guess I'm more of a "stroller writer." It's tough for me to move on from a paragraph if I know something's not right. That was the experience with "#InMemoriam." The other piece, though, "Thou Shalt Ride All the Dinosaurs"—that was an unusual drafting process, in that I woke up in the middle of the night, grabbed my notebook next to the bed, and wrote a big chunk of the story in a few minutes. (I remember I didn't turn on the light, so as to avoid waking my partner, and in the morning I discovered I'd written *on top* of another story instead of on a blank page. Deciphering what I'd written later that day was a fun challenge . . .). I did struggle with the ending of that one, though.

VKN: Superimposition at its best! I have done such a thing before too, but not because I was considerate about my lover's sleep. I did it because I wanted to go back to sleep right away after writing. Why did you struggle with ending "Thou Shalt Ride All the Dinosaurs?" What was your educational experience like at Indiana University? Would you recommend pursuing an MFA to other writers? Are MFA programs conductive to "stroller writers"? Or do you feel like its pressure-cookerness gets in the way of writers becoming writers?

TY: I wasn't sure what emotional note to end on, as is often my struggle with endings. I thought it might be too cheesy to conclude it with the boy gazing up at the narrator so adoringly, but ultimately that's what I went for, because that's how little kids are, and because when in doubt, I prefer images of compassion to ones of sadness or isolation.

I'm definitely a product of the academic creative writing model. There are reasons to be critical of it, and it's not the only way to become a writer, but for me the MFA allowed for a tremendous maturation of my writing in a short period of time, and I remain so grateful for everything I learned at IU. I think the best programs teach both craft and something of the "business" of writing, whether that's literary editing / publishing, or how to pitch your work to an agent. All of that would have been difficult for me to grasp on my own. As for being a stroller writer, the MFA does force you to produce a lot of pages, and quickly, but I think it's a good thing! We all have to work against ourselves as writers—although many of us would like to agonize over our sentences for days, at a certain point you just need to produce, and there's nothing as motivating as a firm deadline and a group of classmates waiting to read your work.

VKN: What advice would you give insomniac writers who wish to compose only fantasy pieces in their free time? Do you think insomnia is a great antidote for creating fantastic worlds or does it act more of an impediment? When I don't sleep, I lose my sense of reality.

TY: I think that, yes, the line between real and unreal gets blurred when you're not well-rested: Perhaps there are writers who can capitalize on that and dream up some brilliant fantastic worlds at 3 a.m., in which case, write away! Personally, I'm not a great writer when I'm going through an insomniac spell. It's fascinating to portray insomnia in fiction, though. It allows you to take familiar things and show them through a distorted lens.

VKN: If you were to produce a piece that has a lot of sapphic material, what would you include in that piece? And, how would you go about writing it? What is an excellent lesbian book that you highly recommend?

TY: I would highly recommend *Zami: A New Spelling of My Name* by Audre Lorde. One of the first lesbian books I ever read, and individual scenes and lines still come back to me. Something I especially admire about that book is how [Lorde] investigates the community of women who have influenced her, all different kinds of relationships, all deeply rooted in a particular time and place. I also love how sensual her details are, even small things like describing inanimate objects.

I would want to emulate that expansiveness in a very sapphic piece—sex not just as an act, but as a kind of texture in the room. Maybe that goes back to the poetic impulses we discussed above. And I would want to consider, too, what pressures a lesbian relationship is subject to from outside, and what pressures it's insulated from, because for me that's what the best queer relationships do: a mutual protection from the forces trying to tell you that what you are is not enough. Of course, lesbians can be terrible to each other, too! But right now, I'm pretty invested in portraying positive and healthy relationships between women.

VKN: Where are you now in life? And, where would you like to go with it? And, can you talk a little about your upbringing?

TY: I'm from Upstate New York, a pretty white suburb, although looking back on it, many of my friends were first- or second-gen immigrants. I was raised Catholic; that tension between being gay and identifying with a religion that continues to view this as sinful comes out quite a bit in one of my stories included here. Much like the narrator in that piece, I'm not a devout Catholic, but I've never been able to completely reject Catholicism, either.

Unsurprisingly, I spent a lot of time reading and writing as a kid, and it was in writing that I first gave myself permission to recognize my sexuality. Of course, I had no idea this was what I was doing! I was eagerly writing lesbian sex scenes, and I kid you not: it didn't occur to me I might be gay until years later. I also spent a lot of time playing imaginative games with my neighbors, usually involving a sword or a magic wand. I can really draw a line right from those games to my interest in writing: They were just stories that we play-acted, trying out different characters. My dream remains to write a series of fantasy novels (probably involving swords and magic wands). I realized that I needed a smaller canvas for a first book, but someday I'd like to tackle a big series set in a fully imagined universe à la Lord of the Rings. I have many ideas . . .

After a few years in the Midwest, I've returned to New York to start work as an assistant professor of English. Teaching was never something I felt I *had* to do, in the sense of it being a lifelong dream, but my past year as a visiting assistant professor was enormously rewarding. I just love talking with students about writing, seeing how excited they get when they're allowed to write about things that matter to them. I already said I was the product of an academic creative writing model: Another way to put it is that I've benefited from some really great teachers. I haven't been in academia long enough to promise it's what I want to do for the rest of my life, but I'm hopeful I can be a great teacher to my students.

SKIN AND FLOWERS

Veshalini Naidu

The "Skin & Flowers" series is an interrogation of my own gender and sexuality as a young lesbian, inspired by the poetry of Nayyirah Waheed and Lily Jamaludin. There are four pieces attached from the series that also respond to major events, both personal and national. "Flower Boy" is in response to the murder of T. Nhaveen, a young Indian boy brutally killed by his bullies from school because of his soft nature. "18 Minutes #1" and "18 Minutes #2" were in response to the caning of two women in the state of Terengganu under Syaria Law for "attempted musahaqah (lesbian sex)." The proceedings including the punishment took eighteen minutes in total. The last piece, "There Only Ever Was Love" was when I fell in love with my ex whose friendship and companionship led to this entire series. Till now it serves as this image of hope for me. A moment of peace and safety that, despite all that continues to happen around us, we are not incapable of being and feeling loved.

FLOWER BOY

Veshalini Naidu

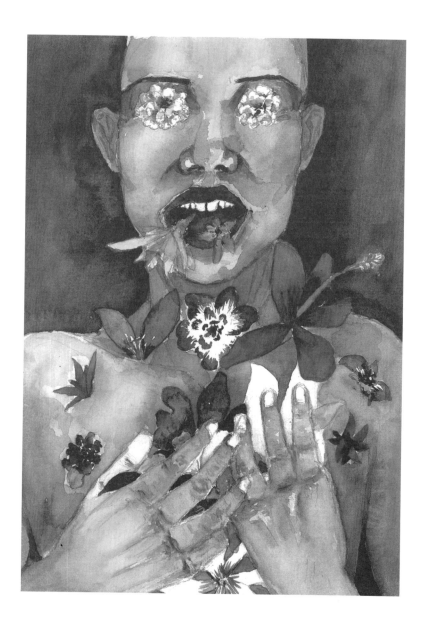

18 MINUTES #1

Veshalini Naidu

18 MINUTES #2

Veshalini Naidu

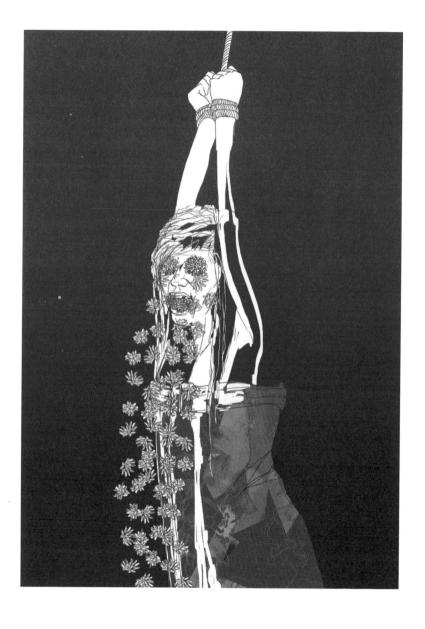

THERE ONLY EVER WAS LOVE

Veshalini Naidu

OUR BODIES UNEARTHED

Kai Tumaneng

when my surname's lost enough muscle to a white mouth,
i'll scoop the wounded limpness of it into my palms, bathe
it with malunggay in broth, pour it into a pot, set it to boil,
let the steam breathe its syllables back into themselves.
when all the similes about soft finger foods finally
lift from our skin, when the olives and almonds
are tucked away into the pantry, you can take
what's left of me. we can teach each other another
cartography, liberated from a voyeur's ink, the balls
of my hands walking the bared bridge of your back,
the moles on your bicep rising as islands unmapped. skirts
will drop and our bodies unearthed will stretch over fields.
we'll shout the sky down, make it scared to smother
us. the oiled veins of our hair will wrap into brambles,
the crooks of our elbows will lengthen into fault lines.
when we've shoveled enough rubble upon the farces
of our smallness, we'll name the sun our second lover.

THE FLOWER STRAINS THE WORLD

Jessica Kieran

It all begins with a seed. Embraced by soil.
Buoyed by water. Nurtured by the darkness,

unseen by all
but the ovule's heart. As she sheds her mortal shell, vulnerable
she reaches to
the depths, stretching

her limbs, spirit, and intellect, digging, burying her
heart's yearning,
crystallizing her intent, wishing

to bet
her life and future on this one wish.

That she be a challenger.

So she rises. Blasts through mother earth's crust, calling for the
world

to take heed.

For here she is.

Tested before the world even knew her.

Pressured by the sun's scorching rays, from the moon's freezing
frost, by the river's flooding purge, overrun by other seeds. Prey to
foraging creatures.

Still. From the river, she grabbed nutrients from foreign lands, and
from the sun she absorbed

warmth for the cold nights. She slipped from the teeth
of predators and found new

ground. Fertile. Won by her tenacious will.

Nothing given, everything taken. By her

right of challenge.
Every wish, every intent, each battle, the seed grasped and
scratched and
punched. Her
strife. Her battle cry. Her

ever-reaching body. Her very ambition.

And thus:
she becomes an aspirer.

Her wishes spread.
Hope rippling, billowing, and heaving. Settling inside
wayward hearts.

Taking root. Sprouting.
Pumping her
strife, her intent, and her nurturing essence into your very marrow.

Into their very marrow. Until a garden grows.

Urging. Hurry, she says.

You can see. You can feel.

The pressure of the earth's mantle. The beating of her salty

blood. Her anger, her
sorrow, her

despair.

You can know. Learn.
Strive.

Bloom. Blast open

against locusts, heat waves, blizzards, drought. Battle against
brambles, whipped by

branches. Stabbed by thorns.

You can fight. Pick up the right
to be a challenger.

It all begins with a seed.

So that a flourishing garden remembers the flower
that strained the
world.

SHE IS NOT A FLOWER

Samirah Boomi

Do you see the Dandelion as a flower or weed?
When you need her power, you free her seeds
Into cold wind, & pray she will lend
A divine intervention in the sway of her spine.
As she moves with the wind, your tension unwinds.

Like a wildfire, she multiplies by day,
till one day, you suspect she's gone astray.

Then, her same raw power
leaves you with a sour taste,
You cower and uproot her in haste,
Discard her as waste, to only make place
for women you perceive as flowers.

SHE IS NOT A "BAD" ASIAN DAUGHTER

Samirah Boomi

They claim "Bad" Asian daughters are family dividers,
but "Bad" Asian daughters are Pan-Asian fighters.
We reclaim the pain, erase the shame.
We will not win, we'll break the game.

LOTUS

Stephanie Wickham

Model: @lim_g_le2
Hair & makeup: @liviamilazzo_makeupartist
Photography and editing: @marklambertphotography
Designed and made by @teacupapparel (all Instagram accounts)

Artist Statement

The lotus flower is one of the most sacred flowers in east Asian culture. Symbolizing spiritual enlightenment as well as rebirth, it is seemingly flawless despite growing in muddy rivers, and re-blooms every morning unscathed. An object of divine energy, it is often depicted with mighty figures and spiritual beings. The layers of the lotus flower are reimagined in the elements of a classic Chinese cheongsam with a contemporary twist. Frog clasps, gold bias hems, and plum blossom brocade cultivate a spring collection with a layered mandarin collar embrace.

FROM POURS POUR [SEE THE MOON]

Kimberly Alidio

see the moon
beautiful no
luminously expand

mirror faces

blue hoodie
disappear

possibility

may not be

margin of error

shines

light ordinance

night darkness

instruments

fuse sensuality

no

moon   transact

stockpile   habitus

habits

trust
mystery
alive

cocoon
courting

FROM POURS POUR [WALL SMALL BONE]
Kimberly Alidio

wall

small   bone

score

touch

gravity

grief

puncture

mildew

head

ache

arrive

spouse

scrim

sky   curve

open

I mean

anti

matter

dense

whistle

MY HAPPY PLACE

Mi Ok Song

IN CONVERSATION WITH VI KHI NAO

Mi Ok Song

VI KHI NAO: One of my favorite visual pieces of yours has the following title, "A Day in a Life." The reason why I love this piece so much is because it combines your poetic impulses/depth with your visual acuity. Can you talk a little about the seed of conception and how long it took you to create it? And, your current preference for what kind of medium you prefer to make your visual pieces?

MI OK SONG: I participate in a Wednesday morning drawing group of live figures (both female and males) for three hours

with my artist friends. I draw while others paint or sculpt in clay. I have been doing this seriously since 2008. I drew the figure in the piece you mentioned in about twenty minutes, just the outline in ink, then went home and finished the drawing in a few hours, incorporating the hours of the day (sunrise/dawn, blue sky, sunset/dusk and night time) as "A Day in the Life" of a woman/ everywoman. I often take line drawings of figures I draw in my group, then take it home, think about the concept of what images

I want to incorporate, and go from there. I prefer black ink pen for the outline & use colored pens for the images, plus white gel pen for highlights and white. My work has evolved from line drawings (of figures), to incorporating more images, to now where the entire piece of paper is covered. My drawings take anywhere from a few hours to several days to complete.

VKN: Yes, I have noticed this evolution on your Instagram page where you showcase some of your artistic productions. As I viewed your work across several days, I noticed that I was particularly drawn to the way you humanize landscapes such as in "Dwelling" and "Home," not just literally, but also figuratively.

And, how you have a sensual way of textualizing animals, nature, plants in your work and making them so seamless. Do you consider yourself more of a figurative artist? Or where in time do you feel your work vocalizes/expresses its philosophical or artistic self best? And, do you feel anachronistically indifferent to time, itself?

MOS: I consider myself more of a figurative artist, as well as more illustrator-like, which I used to feel was insulting in my work being perceived as such, but really, some illustrations are quite exquisite and so I am not insulted as much. The most important element for me as an artist is that my work transcends genre and categorizing, and more importantly, that viewers can imagine they are traveling on some magical journey of discovery, seeing details they haven't noticed before and being amused and charmed by them.

VKN: Who are some of your favorite figurative paintings/ artists? And, what is it about them or their work that you find so compelling?

MOS: I like Frida Kahlo, though some of her work is a bit harsh for me; I like her conceptualization, not necessarily her technique. I like Rosa Bonham and Mary Cassatt as artists.

VKN: If you are not drawn to Kahlo's technique, are you drawn to Bonham and Cassatt's then? I always was so drawn to Cassatt's maternal constitution. Her attention to human digits, of children. Like some of your art pieces as well. I noticed your attention to hands, feet, ankles. What other human body parts do you wish to study in depth?

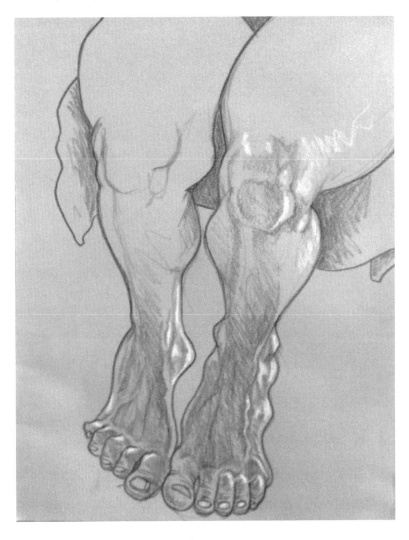

MOS: My focus on hands, feet, and faces is most important to me, because I think they are the most difficult to draw of the human figure. I exaggerate the sizes of hands and feet, which I believe strengthens the drawing. I also pay attention to leaving genitals out, as I feel that a drawing can be more sensual without being sexual, in the implication rather than the obvious.

VKN: I noticed although you do omit certain erogenous zones, some of them are very beautifully and methodically implied as in "A Moment's Glance"—where the skin/texture of the penguin matches a woman's private opening. Was this intentional or was it an afterthought? How do you usually guide your intellectual or aesthetic eye to a particular destination in the end? Or is it more of an organic process?

MOS: Oh, that was purely accidental but a successful accident, I suppose. I do make more of a concerted effort to have my images situated on the drawing so the eye travels all over the surface of the drawing. My sea creature series was a phase obviously, but at the time, it was fun to do.

VKN: I love your pelagic sense of humor. Especially the drawings where fish and sea creatures move freely and isolatingly (at times) and minimally (at times) in your visual works. They feel magical because you have transposed or superimposed them outside of their aquatic context and allow them to swim on a tankless space called carpet or just streets. One of my favorite aquatic pieces of yours is "Koi Dance." Can you talk about this piece? Are you a fan of koi? What is your favorite fish or sea creature?

MOS: "Koi Dance" was a series of three-minute poses of the same figure. All done in ink, drawn directly onto the paper. This was successful as a composition, as I didn't have to reposition the figures when I went home to complete. I fell in love with koi fish as an image to draw, with their bright colors and flowing movement. I am a fan of koi fish, and my favorite fish or sea creature is penguins (they have such character and personality); and I love the fish I did in "Beneath the Surface," as they were so different and colorful.

VKN: Have you done any pieces that are sapphically based? Portraits of two women in an erotic/emotional relationship with each other or with a particular landscape you have in mind for them?

MOS: I have not done pieces that are sapphically based. I have drawn two female figures embracing but they were not erotically posed. If the opportunity presents itself, I will do this, but trying to make this happen seems contrived and this has not happened organically for me, since most of the figure models are singular.

VKN: I can see how that may pose a problem. If an opportunity presents itself, would you be interested in exploring it visually? And, how about your poetry? Have you been able to capture the erotic/romantic pose between two women lovers?

MOS: I wrote one poem, "Astronomy," about (lesbian) sex. It's been published previously.

VKN: Are you happy with it? Why the title "Astronomy"?

MOS: "Astronomy" is a symbolic title for the terminology I used in writing this poem involving sex between two women. It's the only erotic poem I have ever written or gotten published. Happy with it? I am happy it was published. I can email it to you if you want to read it.

VKN: Why do you want your work to transcend genre? And, what does that mean?

MOS: I don't know if my work is anachronistically indifferent to time itself. If you mean if I think my work is timeless? No, I do not think my work is timeless.

VKN: Not timeless, but that it may exist outside of time or in a different time than it is originally designed to be. And, why do you think your work is not timeless?

MOS: My work is not timeless due to some of my images incorporating machinery, like vehicles (in "Dwelling" and "A Vintage Vacation").

VKN: How long have you been living in Warwick? And, working in Providence. What do you do? How do you feel about the New England area? What brings you there?

MOS: I have lived in Rhode Island since 2005, first Providence, then Warwick. I work in Providence as an LICSW, where I treat clients with opiate addictions at a Suboxone clinic (near Brown and RISD). I work there three weekdays and do my drawings at home.

VKN: What is your work like? Can you talk a little about your experience with treating your clients? Do you often involve creativity in your therapeutic work? Or is it a separate part of your social entity?

MOS: I am a strong believer of compartmentalization and boundaries. I keep my creativity separate from my therapeutic work. Most of my clients don't know I am an artist unless they mention that they draw or like art in their lives. Then I support them fully, disclose that I am an artist, and encourage them to continue drawing as therapy for themselves. I also support writing poetry, journaling, crafting, and any other creative outlet to assist their recovery. One or two of my clients have seen my artwork and only when I show it to them. They do not have access to my FB or Instagram, as I choose anonymity as a therapist with my clients.

VKN: Can you talk about your "Mother Earth" piece? Did the woman figure emerge out of your imagination? Or born from limning a model? One of her breasts is the sun and her hair is a bundle of floating clouds. And, her skin is left untouched. I did not expect her veins to flow rivers, but she is sitting on an earth chair. I love the simplicity of the piece. Were you responding to our current ecological culture? Or was there a deeper message you wish to communicate with her and the painting's existence?

MOS: "Mother Earth" was another live figure drawing model. I drew the outline of her there and then went home and finished the colors. I like the fact that her breast is the sun, representing life, warmth, and heat. The chair was supposed to be fire or dusk as her hair is daylight/sky, and her torso is dark/starlit sky. I was experimenting and stopped when I thought the drawing was complete.

VKN: How do you know when your work is complete? What gives it away? What invites? What intuitive power do you use, or how do you access that instinct to know when something is finished?

MOS: Knowing when to stop and consider it finished is half of the battle. Many artists overwork their pieces. For me, it is intuitive.

For example, "Flight of Ideas" was intended to have the entire sky in blue, but I stopped when it was only partially finished. It was knowing when to stop, and the drawing was more interesting with an only partially finished sky in blue. I consider the negative space as important as what I draw. What to leave out is equally as important.

VKN: Your work, like a fish, does not stay still. It moves quickly through different textual realities. Some of your pieces move through a very majestic, minimal state, like "Sister Moon," before accelerating towards polychromatic themes as in "Paradise Found"—do you have a magnum opus you are working towards?

MOS: "Paradise Found" was completed after "Sister Moon." "Paradise Found" was completed at my figure drawing group. "Sister Moon" was drawn at a Tuesday afternoon portrait group. So the portrait group is clothed humans and the figure group is nude humans, thus contextually different, static vs. fluid, moving vs. sitting. I am not sure what you mean by magnum opus? Please explain.

VKN: Like a masterpiece. A piece that is an advance, bold accumulation of all of your life's work, and it exists in one piece. It's a piece that encapsulates the entire composition of your existence. Etc. Some of us work in small pieces across time in order to prepare us for a major painting. Like Picasso's *Guernica*, for instance. He did many cubistic drawings before advancing towards something massive. Are you working towards such ambition?

MOS: I have no magnum opus at the moment, but I hope that I learn from each drawing I complete, improving the quality and vision of each drawing as my technique becomes stronger. I have a vision for my artwork, which now incorporates humans and animals, landscapes, climate, social commentary (I hope). And since I draw, not paint, my drawings are complete as they stand rather than focusing on completing some *big* piece. I have thought of doing triptychs (three panels and two panels), but some of my drawing are companions to one another. I have also considered drawing larger than 18 × 24, which is more ambitious but not necessarily better.

VKN: You are also a talented poet. Your poem "Heart Murmur" is quite an experience for me to read. How did that poem arrive to you? Did it take long for you to produce?

MOS: I wrote the poem "Heart Murmur" in 1995 before I returned to South Korea to search for my birth mother. When I found her in 1997 while living in Korea, I found out that she did have a heart murmur. Interestingly enough, I wrote the poem after my doctor informed me that I had a heart murmur. It was profound enough for me to write the title down, which always comes first. The poem followed a few weeks later and took a few hours to write.

VKN: My favorite part of this poem—let me excerpt it for you:

I was told
that my heart beats differently—

it's not like a normal one.
Something like it skips
or echoes—something

like that. Tell me

What happens when it echoes? Would you ever want to make an art or visual piece that captures this echo? This skipping?

MOS: I have thought about drawing companion visualizations to my poems but haven't pursued it as I feel it may be too redundant and self-indulgent. Who really wants to see my poems as visual drawings? More importantly, I haven't felt drawn to draw my poems out in an organic manner. As I said before, the titles of my poems and drawing present themselves to me. I hold onto the title (of poem or drawing) for days or weeks, then start.

VKN: Samuel Beckett translated quite a few of his own works from French to English. Although I haven't read his translations, I get the feeling that he would do a better job of translating his work than another translator. When your heart leaks, and it enlarges your heart each year from that leak, does your heart ever feel like a broken faucet that drips water? Would you like it to echo less?

MOS: My heart echoing due to a heart murmur informs my artwork and creativity in that I see differently as an artist and a social worker, and a writer and a poet, just as my heart beats differently (than anyone else's). I like that aspect and I would not like my heart to echo less.

VKN: I love taking the bus from Providence to Newport. It's a day trip. With your work so intimately close to the ocean and its sea creatures, which part of Rhode Island do you love spending time at? Can you talk about this "Shoreline" piece? Did you draw this from memory? Or is it from the same method you use where you fill it in later after you have measured its contour(s)?

MOS: "Shoreline" was a drawing I did from a figure, then went home and finished the colors. The figure took twenty minutes, and the completion was an hour or so. My sister lives in Little Compton. I grew up with her and my family there during the summers. We lived in New Jersey until 1975, when my father retired and relocated to Little Compton permanently. I attended high school in both Portsmouth and Middletown. I both love Little Compton for the beauty and the ocean, and hate Little Compton for the horrible high school memories.

VKN: Have you dabbled in filmmaking? I believe you would make an excellent filmmaker. Your eyes for certain details. Your sense of color and thematic symmetry. The way you view the pelagic life.

MOS: I took one filmmaking class in art school and loved it but never pursued it.

FIRST TIME

Jacenne Chloe

her hands slide over my body like
a sculptor working on her next creation.
with every moan and hot breath she
transforms me into a masterpiece.
she doesn't stop until she hears a symphony

She changes careers as smoothly as I
flip my preferred sexual orientation

COST OF COMFORT

Elisha Chen

a light in the hallway, open doors, and
freshly folded laundry. you wonder the price,
counting spare change in sleepless nights
and guilty thoughts

a warm couch, late night company, and
borrowed winter clothes; some things are free,
though they cannot understand
you still have a debt

LOVELY

Elisha Chen

I think there is something missing
in the idea of the skin. I wait for
metaphors, but they evade me.

I've been told of intimacy in heat,
melting into one another, joining streams
into a river of need.

I can't find the beauty in
proximity. I imagine two slabs of clay,
a gray mess of disappearing boundaries.

You are borders filled in; we are parallel lines.
I think maybe a lack doesn't always
require wanting.

I want you to take my hand.
I don't need metaphors to know
that would be enough.

NOT CAROLINE AT ALL

Elisha Chen

once i met a girl with hair the color of
night skies and dreams
she laughed about loneliness and said sometimes
people who love you hurt you

the world seems bigger under the stars
until you run away from them
remember when you reach the edge of the world
it was always this small
—which is to say sometimes you run so far
you find what you left behind

to the girl who has been to the bottom of the well
it was not the wish at fault, rather
the idea that what you got was
anything like what you asked for

IN CONVERSATION WITH VI KHI NAO
Elisha Chen

VI KHI NAO: These poems read like abstract details, like micro-epiphanies hidden in sagacious pills of deep reasoning and experiencing, of your interior ruminations. They arrive from a place of sound erudition and logic that is steadfast and that takes metaphorical leaps without resorting to obvious metaphors. Did you intend for them to arrive in such an encoded, enclosed fashion? As if they appear to be inaccessible, but they are quite accessible, at times, if we read them enough times. How did you intend for them to be in the world?

ELISHA CHEN: I think in some manner I did intend for them to sound that encoded, mostly because the metaphors and imagery I use are very personal and based off of specific experiences in my life. I believe they are accessible in the sense that I don't believe my experiences are necessarily unique, because I'm sure that everyone has experienced in some ways the things that I have, but I did intend for the personal nature of such details to be a bit vague at first. Mostly I think that a lot of the meaning in the imagery I choose are things that people might be able to relate to, and if they can't, however they relate to them is equally important.

VKN: What specific experiences in your life were you referring to, Elisha?

EC: Mostly I draw on my relationships with friends and family members. I think a lot about the kinds of love I have experienced in my life and the ways that people show that love. For my poems "the cost of comfort" and "Lovely," I really focused on that love and tried to imagine my friend's and family's possible perspectives on love. My third poem, I actually drew a lot of the imagery and metaphors from the movie *Coraline*, which is something I'm sure many people have watched. It's really covered in references, and a lot of the metaphors I used are just extensions of how I felt when I saw them in the movie.

VKN: Also, your poems are minimal without being cold. Did you wish to invoke distance, yet appear soft—as in not muted nor restrained, but clear and lucid? There is also empty space, long slants of light in your work, in the way I experience your perception of the world. Is there an artist or architect, live or dead, who most resembles your poetry visually? Who would that be?

EC: I don't intentionally try to make my poetry minimalist, though I can see how that would happen simply because of how I use poetry to work through emotions that I might not know how to process in the moment. I think by trying to distance myself from my thoughts, I just happen to create this sort of minimalism. I don't really know many artists, if I'm honest, but minimalist art has always been my favorite. I always loved the way the simplest techniques can explore such complicated thoughts and imagery. Or also how you can often simplify very complex ideas into something that appears to be easy and simple.

VKN: Your poem "Lovely" opens very invitingly with the following: "I think there is something missing / in the idea of the skin." How did this line arrive to you? And, why did you title it "Lovely"? The word "lovely" is a little bit casual in a foxy way here, but the rest of the poem feels both very abstract and philosophical at the same time. As if you are trying to measure the material of a perception or sensuality by describing the things around it.

EC: The first line of the poem is actually the first part I came up with that gave me the idea for how I wanted the rest of the poem to go. I had wanted to write a love poem for quite some time but had always struggled with it. I was trying to read love poems for a while to get inspiration, and I remembered reading a poem about making love to someone and how poetic it sounded, and I just thought that it would be interesting to write a poem about being unable to find sex as beautiful or poetic. I guess the title just came from the feeling of warmth in intimacy and caring about someone. A feeling that is so simple and sweet, I thought it was appropriate that the name be similarly uncomplicated.

VKN: What love poems were you reading? What were they like? And, why do you think you had always struggled with writing one?

EC: Oh, I don't actually remember anymore. They weren't very impactful or very inspiring, mostly because I couldn't really relate. The specific poem that talked about sex being poetic wasn't even fully a love poem. There was just one line that made me think about the lack of beauty that I find in sex and how I wanted to make this inability to find it beautiful satisfying in itself. I always struggled because as much as I love people, I've never been in a romantic relationship. I also struggled a lot with trying to write a love poem that didn't sound cheesy or overdone, because it never really felt genuine.

VKN: What is your creative ritual like, Elisha? Are you a full-time poet? What are some of your other interests?

EC: I mostly write about specific experiences that I have that make me consider my life that came before that moment. Also, challenging myself to write something that I haven't before is where some of my poems came from, such as "Lovely." I always start with a specific line or stanza that almost summarizes the emotions behind the poem, and then try and build around that by padding the poem with thoughts that surround the main idea. I am not a full-time poet, though I do think that would be fun. I enjoy music, and I play the clarinet and piano. I am studying computer science, which is interesting sometimes and difficult other times. I play video games when I can. And I rock climb! Which is maybe my favorite hobby out of all of them, except for poetry of course.

VKN: And, what are you working on now? And, how is it coming?

EC: Right now I don't really have a main focus for a specific work, though I am trying to write some more. I have two ideas going around in my head, but I've been struggling with actually finishing them. I probably need to get back into writing more, since I've been a little busy lately and haven't really had the time or energy to think more on those ideas. I also am thinking of trying to send out more poetry that I've already written. I've chosen the poems already, so now I just need to come up with where I want to send them.

VKN: In terms of laundry, what is your favorite article of clothing that you love folding? Or perhaps you do not enjoy folding at all. Your poems give me the impression that each poem is an origami piece and you are trying to bend straight lines into us so that we may see the shape or diction of your perception.

EC: I like shirts! Folding is fun most of the time, as long as I have the patience for it. T-shirts are always the nicest because they're some of the easiest and also end up looking tidy, but I really like the appearance of all shirts when they're folded. I do really like straight lines and neat borders, and also the way that when you fold a shirt, the pattern or design is always right in the center. Very convenient for when you're picking out something to wear.

VKN: What is holding you back from being in a romantic relationship? Do you wish to be in one? Sor Juana Inés de la Cruz writes exquisite love (sapphic?) poems and she was a nun!

EC: I do want to be in one just a little, though I'm not exactly looking for a relationship. Mostly I'm waiting to grow up a bit and maybe mature a little more before I try and dedicate myself to anyone. I'm at a point in my life where things are very likely to change, and I am very likely to change, which might not be too conducive for a stable relationship. I'm also maybe not the best at dating. I tried it once and it almost felt weird to me to be trying to feel romantic feelings. I like the idea of waiting to naturally like someone better.

VKN: That sounds wise. Speaking of acquired knowledge, what book(s) are you reading right now? And, would you recommend it? And, what do you love about rock climbing? Is it similar to writing poetry?

EC: I'm not reading anything currently, though I did finish some books a while back. I reread the book *Chemistry* by Weike Wang, which I absolutely love. That's probably obvious because I read it twice, but it really spoke to a lot of things that I sometimes struggle to write about in my own poetry. I would absolutely recommend *Chemistry*. I almost cried, and one of my sister's friends did cry while reading it, so I know it's not just me. I was also reading some young adult fiction, just for fun. I don't really like to take myself too seriously when I read fiction most of the time. I don't know if I would suggest any of those, but they were good for just a little bit of relaxation. For rock climbing, I love the combination of the physical challenge it presents and also the puzzle of which moves to use. It also has an easy measure of your improvement, since as you improve you get to tackle climbing routes with a higher difficulty rating. It's an incredible feeling when you're stuck on a route, and then a week later you finally manage to finish it. I wouldn't say it's similar to poetry; it's actually probably the opposite. Whereas for poetry I often use a lot of introspecting, in climbing all of the focus is on your body and the way that you manipulate where your weight falls. The focus is on physical matters, whereas poetry focuses on internal, emotional matters. I like how they're dissimilar though, because they give me outlets for both types of thinking.

VKN: Thank you for the Wang recommendation. I will need to check it out. I like literary tears. Do you have a favorite lesbian film? If so, what do you like about it?

EC: I'm honestly not a big fan of most lesbian films. I did like *Disobedience*, which I thought was very good with the pining. *Carol* was also nice, but I am more moderate in my feelings about that one.

VKN: How come? Have you seen Park Chan-wook's *The Handmaiden*? It's one of the more gorgeous lesbian films I have seen lately.

EC: I think that a lot of lesbian films are either very dramatic and kind of sad, or very cheesy and campy. Not that either of those genres are bad, but they're not really the kind of film that I usually enjoy watching. I did actually see a little bit of that one! I read the book and hadn't realized that they'd made it into a film, but I'll have to give it another try. The first time I watched it, I was seeing it with my sister, and she didn't quite enjoy it, so we stopped. Based on how I liked the book, I think I would enjoy the movie though.

VKN: Best not to watch sapphic films with sisters? I did read Sarah Waters's *Fingersmith* and thought the film and book were in indirect conversation with one another in a deep anachronistic and ethnic way. Also, I love the fashion statement in Chan-wook's film. I would just watch the film for the blouses and gloves. Let alone its strident, sensual, erotic sapphic material. I hope you will finish it.

EC: Oh, I don't know, watching sapphic films with her is pretty good. She was the one who actually got me to watch *Carol* and *Disobedience*, which I had avoided because they had seemed very sad. I think that maybe the plot of *The Handmaiden* wasn't her style, which is a little understandable. Their relationship in the beginning does not seem conducive to a romantic relationship. I agree with you! I didn't get too far into the movie, but it looked absolutely gorgeous, honestly. I'll get on that very soon!

LIUXING JOHNSTON

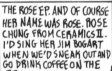

©Lemon Liu Art

CURIOSITY

Fiona Gurtiza

I once dated a girl who had a thousand questions.
Nothing could ever satisfy her burning, unfulfilled desire to learn
    new things
And I felt the same elation of discovery she did
Each time I watched her face light up when another new discovery
    struck her.
She just had to know. *And so did I.*

I tell her it's no wonder she graduated with Latin honors,
But she responds with her customary eyebrow furl
and tosses her hair back like none of her achievements counted.
When we met, I threw her entire worldview off-kilter.
I held her hand and told her there was more to life than seeking
    enlightenment
For its own sake.

She wasn't just a typical overachiever:
From elementary to high school, she held the highest academic
    ranking.
She set the bar up so high and
I always wondered why she constantly belittled herself
When all I'd ever gotten was an award for a spelling bee in the third
    grade.
It turns out that her parents had never told her that they were
    proud of her.

Sometimes, I wonder if this is why she keeps asking questions.
Maybe her quest to find answers would one day tell her
Why she wasn't born as pretty as her younger sister was
Or why her parents disowned her for being in love with a girl.

When I told her that she had a cold case of impostor syndrome
Her face didn't light up the way in the way I had memorized
Whenever she learned something new.

I've never liked asking questions.
You never know what unpleasant truths you could uncover.
And I've been trying to make up for years of ignorance
By teaching her that some answers can be unsatisfying
Because some questions only exist to spawn further confusion.
When I asked her why she loved me
She opened her mouth a fraction, blinked a few times
And stepped back slowly.
She didn't know.

They say in the age of information, ignorance is a choice.
Relentless news cycles and deep ideological divides create pressure
And the worst that could happen is not knowing where we stand.
But love is different. And I knew because I had found her kryptonite.
"I don't know," she told me
And these words are tantamount to the three most spoken words
Between starry-eyed teenagers falling in love for the first time.

Love is unpredictable and unquantifiable.
Sometimes we feel the way we do, not knowing why or how, as I do.
Still, her curiosity is a perpetual, unstoppable force
And to this day I find myself asking why.

HOMEBODIES

Sierra Perrett

To put it lightly, apartment hunting is my own personal hell. Tiled floors, carpeting, hardwood—after a while it all blends together. Without Kiernan's hand in mine, I might have melted into the crown molding already. I grab another freshly baked chocolate chip cookie. This time the chocolate melts into my hand as I break off half for Kiernan. She takes it and kisses my cheek.

"You two make such a cute couple," the realtor says. She just says it to be perky—the most crucial part of her job, and yet I can't help but beam. "This neighbourhood is perfect for couples. Two bedrooms with lots of natural light, and the nightlife is great. It'd be a good fit."

"We'll let you know," Kiernan says back, but she sounds off. She drags me out and shuts the door before I have the chance to ask about it. Now I'm sure she's off. She always slams doors, though she's never explained that decision. Always calls it one of her quirks. Maybe there isn't a story behind it.

"You didn't like it?" Starting with this might get her to open up a bit. One thing always leads to another with her. Another quirk, but I love it.

"Huh? Oh. I don't know. I liked the red one better."

There wasn't a red one. The closest was orange and it was hideous. She's still off, like another switch needs to be flipped before she's my girlfriend again, and for some reason, it hasn't been. She can try to bury it all she wants, but after two years together I'm fluent in her.

She takes off her scarf and wraps me in it. "Let's just think about it. Not make any rash decisions?" I find myself nodding. And because she's fluent in me too, she says, "I'm fine, Grace. Really."

But what does fine even mean? Fine exists in the limbo between shitty and wonderful except it doesn't mean anything, not really anyways. It's only there to set someone's worries at ease. It never works on me, especially not when it comes to Kiernan.

She doesn't look at me the entire drive back. I know she loves people watching, but never this much. She doesn't even point out the dogs that walk by or roll down the window so the breeze blows in her face. Or make a comment about how all this neighbourhood needs is one more Starbucks before it turns into Urbanized Hell. The other building blocks are all there: Lululemon mom gangs pushing strollers, the faded Neighbourhood Watch sign, dads that yell to each other over shared fences. But Kiernan says nothing. She never misses an opportunity like that and yet, she does.

Knowing she's off doesn't automatically mean I know what's wrong. Sometimes I wish it did. Everything would be easier. I want to ask, but Ross is on my stoop when we get home. Somehow the second Tuesday of the month became our day. Not that it's anything special, all we do is drink tea and watch a movie we loved when we were kids.

Kiernan wouldn't have even come if she hadn't needed to grab her uniform before her shift. By now, we practically live together—we both have drawers at the other's place, but somehow whatever we need is never where we are. It is a pain in the ass and a big part of why we want a new place together.

She kisses my cheek before she goes, but everything happens in a flash. And I'm left with this weird feeling—like everything around me is in technicolor while I'm stuck in black and white. I lean into it for a moment. Ross is preoccupied trying to land popcorn in my empty cup of chamomile anyway. I don't think he notices until he tosses a piece at my ear.

"Jesus. What was that for?" I ask.

"You were drifting again. Couldn't think of a better way to get your attention. Plus, now you've got a snack."

"I was not drifting." Okay, maybe I was.

He squints, clearly not buying my awful lie. Not that I'd expect him to. "Jesus, Grace. We've been friends for like fifty Nicholas Cage movies. You think that means I can't tell when you're keeping something from me? This has never worked before. What is it?"

"Nothing."

"Okay, Pinocchio. Don't tell me. You know I'll find out." He turns to me and searches my face for the smallest crack in my façade. When you've known someone that long, the basic rules of friendship go out the window and you can do whatever the fuck you want. Now Ross pokes my cheek and that's all he needed to get it.

"Kiernan's being weird," I say.

"She's always weird."

"No, this is different. She's not telling me something."

"Your superpower's still intact then?"

"And useless if she keeps freezing me out." I grab some popcorn from the bowl on his lap as a distraction.

"Since when won't she talk to you?" Ross asks.

"Since now apparently. It's like there's a bad connection between us or something."

"Holy bad superpower, Batman!" Almost anything from the Bat Cave would be better than this. "And you actually asked her what was wrong?"

I roll my eyes. "Yeah, because now I'm a therapist."

"Lesbians are something else."

"Like you'd ask Nick what was wrong."

"Yeah, I would. And your life would be a lot easier if you did the same."

I don't say anything back, only stare at my hands. Ross places his on top, gives mine a squeeze. "Hey, wanna watch *The Princess Bride*?"

"As you wish."

"There's my girl."

The Princess Bride has always been my go-to movie for when I need something mindless, but tonight it falls flat. I register the scenes, but nothing really sticks. Buttercup kept reminding me of Kiernan. They're not even similar—unless you count the blonde hair and the smile that would make anyone's heart stop. Cheesy, I know, and she would've hated the comparison. She never needed anyone to save her, especially not a prince.

I don't know why Ross lets it play for so long. Maybe it's his crush on Wesley. He finally stops it in the big battle after they invade the castle. Right as Inigo Montoya raises his sword against Rugen.

"That's the best part."

"I know it is, which is why I'm surprised you're not paying more attention," he says, then tosses the remote onto the coffee table. It lands on the corner and tumbles off. "For once, *The Princess Bride* can't fix everything."

I reach for the fallen remote.

"Grace, come on."

"Grace, come on where?" Kiernan asks. What the hell? Has she been here the whole time? No, her coat's still on. "How was the movie day, love?" she asks, and that static feeling is back again. Kiernan has a thing with pet names. Not all of them, only "love." Says it makes her feel like an old English woman. So why did she say it?

Ross cuts in before I can turn it over in my mind. "Fine, darling. How was work?"

The rest of their conversation fades away like they've gone through a tunnel. And next thing I know, Ross has his coat on and stands up. I'd almost forgotten his superpower is making an exit in under a minute. "Catch you later, Grace, and you too, sweetheart."

Kiernan cringes. "That sounds so Victorian."

"Apologies, m'lady." He bows. Tries to maneuver around the couch, hits his knee against the corner, plays it off, and makes it to the door with minimal limping. Everything he does is a performance whether he wants it to be or not.

Kiernan collapses next to me on the couch. Buries her head in my neck. Her hair tickles my face. God, it's hard to keep thoughts in my head like this.

"Jesus, that shift was killer. Can we stay like this for a while?"

"Yeah." No.

Ross gave me the chance except I don't know how to take it. I'm about to fold, I can feel my thoughts collapsing in on themselves. How the hell do I start? Fuck, I hate this.

If the situation were reversed, Kiernan would know exactly what to say. How to hold my hand for support without making it seem like a confrontation, what cup of tea I needed to push through this, even the right kind of blanket to wrap around us for the conversation itself.

"What is it?" she asks, not because she's fluent in me, but because she always seems to know. "Are you alright?"

"I'm fine."

"Okay, then what is it? You're fine, I'm fine, Ross looked fine." But once again, fine doesn't mean nothing's wrong.

"You're not okay."

"I'm fine."

"Fine isn't okay."

"But I am." It comes out shakily like the tremor before an earthquake.

I reach up and stroke her hair. Tuck a piece behind her ear. "No, you're not."

She sighs, and her frail façade collapses when she exhales. "God, it's just like . . ." For a second, we're both trapped in this weird beat of silence. "I've felt so fucking body-snatched lately and I don't even know why. I look in the mirror and I don't recognize who that person is and my hands don't feel like they're a part of me and I don't know how to tell anyone—hell, even you—any of this without making it sound like I've fucking lost it. I know how this sounds. But that's the only way it makes any sense and that's barely."

I try to reach for her hand, but she won't give it to me. "Ki."

She shakes her head. "I can't. This entire thing is too fucked up. If I can't get it to make sense to myself, all hope of that happening with someone else is lost."

"You could've said something. I always wanna help you."

She runs a hand across her face. It comes back damp. "I know. I know. I'm not good at talking about the shit that bothers me. I don't know why I'm that way."

I turn her face towards me. Tears hang off her cheekbones. "Talk to me. It doesn't have to be anything more than word vomit."

Kiernan takes my hand now, interlocks our fingers, and squeezes them. "I love you so much, Grace. You're the sun, the stars, the moon, everything and more. You turn my world. And you know all of that already, but I need you to know we're good. We're great. This is . . ." Another strange silence grabs us both. "It's about me and I hardly know what it's about. It's like this is Kiernanmageddon and I don't have a clue what caused it or how to stop it. Or maybe I know exactly what it's about and I don't want to say it."

This time I squeeze her hand. I don't know what she's thinking, at least not yet, but this is good enough.

"Remember Ross's friend from work? Lex? They were at his birthday party last month and you made a Lex Luthor joke and they actually laughed?"

I nod, but something's still missing. Like we're trying to build a puzzle without some of the pieces.

"I think I'm like Lex. I don't know, maybe I'm not. I could be something else entirely, but this feels more right than I have in a long time." Kiernan's fingers start to tap along the back of my hand. I bring them up to my lips and kiss them.

"I love you. I wanna start every single day with you for as long as you'll have me. I'm in love with this Kiernan right in front of me. No one else. I'm not going anywhere."

Kiernan leans their head against mine and they're finally clear. No traces of static left.

Q&A

Abigail Del Fierro

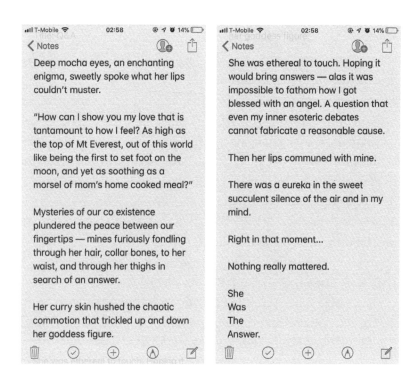

Deep mocha eyes, an enchanting enigma, sweetly spoke what her lips couldn't muster.

"How can I show you my love that is tantamount to how I feel? As high as the top of Mt Everest, out of this world like being the first to set foot on the moon, and yet as soothing as a morsel of mom's home cooked meal?"

Mysteries of our co existence plundered the peace between our fingertips — mines furiously fondling through her hair, collar bones, to her waist, and through her thighs in search of an answer.

Her curry skin hushed the chaotic commotion that trickled up and down her goddess figure.

She was ethereal to touch. Hoping it would bring answers — alas it was impossible to fathom how I got blessed with an angel. A question that even my inner esoteric debates cannot fabricate a reasonable cause.

Then her lips communed with mine.

There was a eureka in the sweet succulent silence of the air and in my mind.

Right in that moment...

Nothing really mattered.

She
Was
The
Answer.

MY DUCK

Editha "Aster" Delgado

This is a film still from my first short film, "My Duck," about a young lesbian growing up on a duck farm in rural Philippines. You can find more information about my film here (including the trailer): https://filmfreeway.com/MyDuck.

SHOWER OF LOVE

Editha "Aster" Delgado

I painted "Shower of Love" especially for *Sinister Wisdom*. It shows the attraction, love, and affection between two Asian lesbians, which is rarely represented in art.

INTERNET ROMANCE / 網路浪漫

Peace Wong

Some online crushes
一些線上心跳
Some Internet romance
一些網路浪漫
Some violent ones you have them
一些暴戾愛戀你幻想過的有的沒的
Inside your head
在腦間
So big, so real, so complex
那麼巨大那麼真實那麼繁複
So intense
得令人緊張

Something's cooking up there
有什麼正在發生
Something's cooking up there
有什麼正在醞釀？
So big so great so complex
有什麼美麗想像錯綜複雜
Something so great you have
你擁有過的有的沒有
Inside your head
在腦海

Over the cloud
雲端以上
Inside your head
大腦以內
With all the gals you'd never met
許許多多從未路上相逢的女子，來來

Straight or queer
無論直／彎
Right-handed or left
右撇子／左撇子
Something so great you have them
你擁有過的有的沒的
Inside your head
在腦海

3 inches closer
走近三吋
5 inches back
走遠五吋
3 inches closer
走近三吋
5 inches back
走遠五吋
6 inches closer
走近六吋
8 inches back
走遠八吋

Leave it hanging there
由她

YOUR BODY IS MY CONFIRMATION, AND MINE, YOURS

SKR

* Write a poem that starts with "Her big fat (insert an adjective of preference) cock . . ."

Her big fat caramel cock
Stretches out the walls of my vagina
Revealing the texts hidden in the deep wrinkly grooves
The texts fall off the walls with textured gasps
Voicing their sounds, sounding their voices
With every thrust
Mouths open wide and speak,
This ancient language from the beginning of time

***

* Write a poem in Korean and translate into English. Notice if there are meanings that are mutually un-translatable. Pay attention to the differences or deviances that occur in each poem. Are the two poems the same or different?

그녀의 __ 이 내 안에 들어왔을 때
Conduit
그것은 굵고 딱딱했다.
질 벽을 쫙쫙 다림질하듯 뜨겁게 펼쳐내는 그녀. 그녀의.

.쫄깃한 주름들이 오도독 늘어나면서.
후두둑 후두둑
토도독 알알이
그곳에 새겨진, 알알이 맺혀있던, 숨겨진 말씀들이
떨어져나왔다. 고대문서를 발굴하듯이

파고들고 또 파고들었다.
말씀의 비밀들이 척추를 타고 뇌에 이르러 불을 지폈다.
후두둑 후두둑 두두두둑
무지개빛 색깔들, 네온 오렌지색
내 질벽 주름 속에 숨겨져있던 나
쾌락 속에서 그녀가 일어난다.

When her ___ came inside of me
연결도관

It was big and hard.
She spread out my vaginal walls like a hot iron
Her.
.Supple wrinkles stretched out far and wide. Hoodooduk, hoodooduk
Tododok allari
The hidden words inscribed in the vaginal walls fell out As we
excavated the ancient texts
Deeper and deeper,
The mysteries of the Words climbed up my spine
And inn(en)ervated my brain
Hoodooduk, hoodooduk, doodoodooduk
Colors of the rainbow, neon orange,
Could it be that I am hidden in the vaginal folds?
She wakes up, in pleasure.

* Write a poem in Korean and then translate into English. Examine
if the translated words are standing in rows, stiff and rigid. What
are the things you reveal or conceal in one language or the other?

그녀 안에 들어갔을 때
후두둑 후두둑
주름진 말씀들이 내 손안으로 풍성히 떨어져내렸다.
질벽의 골들이 쫙쫙 늘어났다.

손끝이 울퉁불퉁한 골들을 지나칠 때마다
물오른 말씀들이 황홀한 목소리로 탄성을 지르셨다.
　　　　　　　말씀들은 어린아이처럼 기쁘게
숨어있던 주름골로부터 내 손바닥 안으로
폴짝
뛰어내리셨다.
까르르 까르르
햇살 속에 스스로 드러내는 것이 마냥 기쁜신양 풍만하고
　　　　　　　　　　　달콤한 목소리들이
굽이굽이 이랑마다
스스로를 거둬들인다.
새로이 태어난 촉촉한 생명의 말씀들이
내 안에 석류알처럼 알알이 들어찬다.
나는 더이상 너의 타자가 아니다.

When I went inside her
Hoodooduk Hoodooduk
Groovy Words fell abundantly into my palm.
Supple ridges of her vaginal walls
Stretched
Tips of my fingers strummed her inner textures
And the Words let out gleeful moans
The Words, blissfully jumping into my palm
Leaving their seats of seclusion
Childlike
Happy to reveal themselves in the sun
Sweet, corpulent, and succulent
In every meandering furrow
They penetrate and arrive at the Self
Filling me up like the jewel grains of a pomegranate
　　　　　　　　　　No longer the other

* Write something in Korean based on something that you wrote in English, then translate into English.

내손에 고이 모두은
네게서 온 생명수
타자성이 증발되고 나면
너는 나의, 그리고 나는 너의, 견신례

This Water of Life that came from you,
That I shroud with my palms
When otherization evaporates,
You are my, and I am your, confirmation

NIGHTHAWKS AND HER WIFE

Zodiac River

Such vitriolic sense of romance. Wicked and acerbic, abhorrent and absolutely brusque, tragic, the totality of this disaster is heinous. The glow of the matinal sunshine in your eyes showed me, clearly, obviously, really, the reciprocated glance of a delirious, proverbial woman in trance—such picturesque figure, lovely in looks, but brash in demeanor. Like a demon.

Should I die a thousand deaths before I can usurp your throne, where you sit on diamonds and rubies and my tangled heartstrings; should I say sweet goodbyes to you a million times before I can be your dearest, your darling, your doom?

The bones on your back are like a splendid vista, and grazing my fingers against it is an individual splendor that sins my tongue. This is the anatomy of catastrophe and insolence, and the scathing wound on my lips starts to become effervescent supernovae and spinning galaxies and baneful planets.

When my remains are found, somewhere under the rubbles of your hair, maybe archaeologists would assume that I am yet another case of a Juliet's mistake; a serious stab scar on the chest, right where the heart is supposed to be, open and wide and gaping. But they don't know the truth, nor have they wished to discover. It's the mark you placed on me, within my soul and upon my dreams, as a memento of remembrance, a sign that we were once, in this world and the other, lovers, women that drunk honey from each other's teeth.

This is the essence of what I was so wax so romantic about. Books, songs, love. And then your arrival in this pathetic heart knifed all of the curtains, and suddenly, all the glass, colorful mosaic windows are shining bright. I am suddenly fixated on you. You. Focused on the curves of your lips, obsessed with the sweep of your cheeks. What a dreadful potpourri.

I wish I could write poetry. About the quiet world, the mountains in your eyes, the panorama of the moon as she rises and sets. But do they? We were only enlightened about sunrises and sunsets and the beauty of the phenomenon, but not about the moon, never the moon—this is a despicable tragedy of humanity, and in an event, a single, flawed event: passion and ignorance clash.

Just like us.

XXX

Ayame Whitfield

they show girls with names like mine
in pleated skirts and sailor blouses
hitched up, baring gold-pearl skin
begging to be marked. twintailed black
hair and open mouths and heated breath,
ceramic statues caught mid-climax.

i stop tying my hair like that, and then
i cut it off entirely. *ka-wa-ee*. nightmares
about school uniforms and porn categories
with my silhouette. the stripped women say
yamete, but i don't know what that means.
there are other things i know: *you never*
see fat asian girls. i'm fourteen when i look
in the mirror and think of hanging cow udders
at my own naked reflection. the other
moon-eyed girls have slender legs while my thighs
spill over the edges of the toilet seat, so
i change in the locker room bathroom stall,
elbows knocking the metal divider. i'm
blood-living proof that *asian women love white men.*
half of me a flower and half of me a field
lying quiet and waiting to be plowed. so
patient, because *asian girls are submissive.*
i'm sixteen and i'm trying bravery on and
it fits worse than the swimsuits that i can't
pull past my hips. places and words
that feel like yellow caution tape. i'm not
allowed to want like this. there's a girl
with golden hair and she's the princess i wanted

to be, but laughing shameless.
i hold the girl's hand but i don't dare
kiss her. there are words for what
i know but none of them sound right
with a name like mine.

i learn how to say *stop* in my
mother's tongue. *yamete, kudasai.*
all the words for unwanting that
no one hears. the desires i don't
have a language for.

i dream about being alone in the locker room
with her *adzuki*-red lips on mine, her taste
sweet down my throat, her body
soft against me, just sports bras
and underwear and so much skin, miles
and miles of it, until i'm drowning
in her touch.

IN CONVERSATION WITH VI KHI NAO
Ayame Whitfield

VI KHI NAO: You are a lover of tea, drinking tea, yes? What is your favorite tea, Ayame?

AYAME WHITFIELD: I am! There's a tea shop near where I live that has a really wonderful spiced mandarin oolong tea that I always stock up on when I'm home.

VKN: Why do you love tea so much?

AW: Ever since I was young, my mother would drink a cup of peppermint tea at night, and when she started letting me do the same, it felt like I'd grown up a bit. It's still very soothing for me to make myself a cup of tea in the evening, or any time of day.

VKN: The initial "S" is your middle name, yes? What does it stand for? Do you prefer ASW or AW?

ASW: The S stands for Sumiko, my middle name. I usually sign my poems ASW, but either is fine!

VKN: When did you start collecting polyhedral objects? Do you ever feel that some of your poems are polyhedral in their emotional or ecological intensity?

ASW: Most of the polyhedral objects I collect are dice for Dungeons & Dragons, which I started playing in high school. I got really into collecting pretty dice sometime last summer. And I suppose that every poem I write has a sort of three-dimensionality to it; I usually try to write poems that say more than one thing or deal with more than one topic, or that can be read in a different light depending on how you approach it.

VKN: Can you talk about the birth of "XXX"? How did the poem arrive to you? Did you work excessively hard on it? What do you love most about it?

ASW: I specifically wrote "XXX" for the *Sinister Wisdom* submission call, because I know that being both half-Asian and a lesbian are parts of my identity that shape my poetry, but I'd never explicitly addressed both of those factors in one poem. I wanted to see what writing about that would feel like, and the fact that it ended up being polished enough to submit was a bonus. I started with the lines that ended up concluding the poem, actually, and built the poem around the contrast of that moment of tenderness with everything else explored. It took a few tries to get a poem I really felt satisfied with, and I definitely reworked it more than I usually do with my poems, but in the end I feel like the emotional flow of it works well.

VKN: I don't know how to word this question. But, can you talk more about tenderness and lesbianism and Asianness? Do you feel or know other writers who are able to capture the heart of your (our) Asian desire? If so, who are those? And, why do you think they are so successful at doing so?

ASW: Ocean Vuong's work absolutely kills me with how beautiful and real but tender it can be. He does a lot of things with his writing that I want to be able to do someday, playing with words in such a skillful way but also creating unique and vivid scenes.

VKN: Why do you think he is so successful?

ASW: I think he has a way of taking these deeply personal experiences and opening a window to them, not in a way that makes the reader feel voyeuristic, but in a way that makes the reader—if not understand exactly how it feels to experience such things, to at least feel an echo of that.

VKN: One of my favorite lines from "XXX" starts with the following: "half of me a flower and half of me a field / lying quiet and waiting to be plowed." About that half flower, what kind of flower did you have in mind? And, what kind of a field . . . I don't always think of "field" as in rice or corn field.

ASW: Ah, that line is sort of a self-reference . . . My first name, Ayame, means "iris" in Japanese, as in the flower, and my last name, Whitfield, is probably derived from some variation of "wheat field." I've always been very aware of my name being just as half-and-half (so to speak) as I am.

VKN: I like "Whitfield"—it reminds me phonetically of "wit field." Speaking of fields, I notice that your work is very verdant, meaning nature or the cosmos seems to be an important branch of your poetic composition, and other poems I have read online by you, such as your acute attention to the planets in "The Eight"— can you talk about your pull or proclivity towards such eco or intergalactic materials? Do you feel that "XXX" is an extension of that direction or does it feel like your poetic sexuality is a different sort of beast entirely?

ASW: Natural imagery has always found a way to work itself into my poetry—I think a lot of it has to do with my poetic influences being people like Mary Oliver or the older, more classical poets I read as a child. I think of myself, and the rest of humanity, as being *part of* nature and the natural world rather than separate from it, and that extends beyond this planet, too. That's a concept that I find a lot of poetry in. "XXX" became something a bit different in that I often use natural imagery as something beautiful, whereas for a lot of "XXX" I was focusing on heavier, more artificial things.

VKN: Can you talk a little about the photographic/artistic images on your Instagram page (@avolitorial)? I love how it's a more simplified version of your poetic impulses. Can you talk more about the process of creating these incandescent circular poetry amongst these ecophotographs?

ASW: Social media in general is how I got my start writing poetry—I'm more active on Tumblr, but Instagram is also a place where I tend to post more immediate work. Longer, more polished poems I save to submit to places for possible publication, but I love posting within a community of poets and seeing their reactions to my work and reacting in turn to theirs. The images I use as covers for those poems are mostly just to grab attention, hoping that people will swipe through and read the whole thing!

VKN: What do you think is the most romantic gesture between one lesbian woman and another?

ASW: Honestly, any romantic gestures between lesbians touches me; I saw this video on social media recently where these two women proposed to each other at the same time and I was just . . . sobbing over how beautiful it was. But beyond the grand gestures, I think there's a really underrated romance in the little ways that you can anticipate your partner's needs and desires and be there for them, or just letting them know that they're in your thoughts—like buying their favorite snack for them, stuff like that.

VKN: Have you seen this video, Ayame? (Angela & Ashley's Wedding)

https://www.youtube.com/watch?v=ihvs6yc641c

ASW: I had not but now I'm tearing up, it's so beautiful!

VKN: Who do you think is your ideal reader for "XXX"? Or do you feel that just anyone who identifies herself as lesbian is the ideal reader?

ASW: I think my ideal reader is any woman who understands being fetishized both for her race and her sexuality. I'm in an online group made up of women (or women-aligned people) of color who are lesbian or bisexual, and when I shared parts of this poem with them, the feeling of understanding and support and compassion from them was overwhelming.

VKN: What is your favorite line from "XXX"?

ASW: "there are words for what / i know but none of them sound right / with a name like mine."

VKN: Why is that?

ASW: It points to one of the core emotions in the piece, which is that I've known about lesbian identity for a long, long time, but I never felt like it was something I was allowed to claim as my own, because I'd never seen someone like me do so.

CHRYS1

Light Liu

CHRYS2

Light Liu

CHRYS3

Light Liu

ON STALWART QUEER VIETNESS:
IN CONVERSATION WITH VI KHI NAO

Laura Tran

VI KHI NAO: When I interview people, I usually read everything about them, in preparation. But with you, I thought I would like to start with an emotional, social tabula rasa. What kind of keys would you like me to create in order to open and enter the corridors of your world?

LAURA TRAN: When you say keys, it makes me think more about lenses through which to see people. In this context, I feel like 1) There's nothing to read about me. And 2) I'm not specifically "an artist." But since this is a blank slate, it kinda gives us room to explore more. So, keys/lens: I'm a queer Vietnamese woman living in Portland, Oregon. I grew up in NYC. My parents were never married, and it's a very complex story. But simplified, my parents were refugees from the war, and they fled with a few thousand other people during the fall of Saigon. I'm their last child. I grew up in NYC in the '90s, which was a tumultuous time for the city. I went to public school, was never really "gifted" but always had "potential." This isn't really answering your question specifically, but I think is sort of a gateway to my life.

VKN: Thank you, Laura, for opening this brief historical/cultural/autobiographical box of you for me. It offers many vectors of light to explore the hidden vortexes of your existence. You described yourself in quotes as "an artist." What kind of artist are you? What medium(s) do you work best in?

LT: Well, again, I'm not specifically "an artist." I feel like I've pursued creative outlets, mostly in a hobby-ish way. One example would be ceramics. But the reason why I say "an artist" is because I believe that there a few ways people exist as "artists" and one way is to primarily describe oneself as "an artist," which I would never do. It's not a public endeavor for me. I think that's a very specific line between artists and people who have creative pursuits. My partner is definitely an artist. She is a poet, and she works with several different mediums and it's the core of her identity. I, however, would primarily identify with the work that I do, which is as a small business owner of a local restaurant, navigating the ins and outs of business managing. Very different. But I feel like my identity (my background, my history, my experiences) leans me into this new world of being able to weave my life into stories that I can share with people, which is therefore "art," in a way.

VKN: I don't know many Vietnamese queer women. In the last thirty-nine years, I think you are the second queer Vietnamese woman I have actually interacted with. How did you meet your partner, Laura? Have you always known that you are queer? Is your family accepting of your sexual orientation? Your Vietnamese parents?

LT: I've been with Catie for about two years. We met right before I opened up XLB with my business partner, Jasper. She was subletting a room at my friend's house during the Snowpocalypse of 2017. We met a few months before, and I ended up going to Vietnam for three weeks to travel. She DMed me on Instagram, asking if I ever planned on coming back. I did, and we've been together ever since.

Wow! You've only met two queer Vietnamese people?! One time I wrote a paper for a women and gender studies class, and the prompt was to interview any woman and write a paper about them. I interviewed my mom, and it was the best paper of my life (which is not saying much). I wrote about the experiences of Vietnamese women and how they move through life with four different, uh, virtues. I used this book, and at first glance it seems outdated, but here are the four virtues:

1-. Right Occupation
2-. Right Speech
3-. Right Appearance
4-. Right Conduct

Very similar to Chinese ideals for women as well. The interesting thing I find about this is that you take these virtues, imbue Vietnamese women with them, but then you make them refugees to a different country (US), and then you have the diasporic experience. The internal struggle of trying to fit in your old culture and the new.

I have not always known I was queer. My mother, I believe, tries to actively ignore that part of my identity. My dad is dead, and my parents are strict Roman Catholics. My mom still loves me and is very proud of me as a person in life, but I think in some ways, does she wish I could live a more normal life? Of course. That's why we live here. But I think my upbringing from my mom, a strong independent woman, kind of led me on this path that I'm on. I think I'm queer because through of all my life experiences, I have been enamored by the hard work and endurance of women. Obviously, there is the sexual attraction, but it all begins with the most influential people in my life. My mom as a strong woman. My dad as a powerful, philandering, abusive man.

Can I ask you a question?

Do you identify as queer?

VKN: That I know of. Yes, of course. I am a lesbian Vietnamese woman. I am more lesbian than queer. Queer is too broad for my sexual taste. I am femme. Preferring femme women. I am sexually drawn to men, but only biologically. I don't fall in love with them. And, since I view sexuality as more emotionally erotic than sexually emotional, I highly prefer women. I suppose, if I put my mind to it by removing my heart, I could find happiness with a man, but so is nunhood. Is your Catie Asian? What has your dating experiences like? How do you describe/express your queerness?

LT: Yeah, I thought it was interesting that your call for *Sinister Wisdom* was a call for "Asian Lesbians." I majored in women and gender studies so I have very specific cues when I hear Lesbian versus Queer, and I do believe it has a lot to do with shifting paradigms for identities. I honestly think "queer" is a perfect title, because it gives room for things that are not black and white. I don't know you, and I don't want to proscribe anything to you, but how does one navigate a lesbian identity while simultaneously being biologically interested in men? I think that's one reason "Queer" has become a umbrella term to give room and space to the complicated identity.

My partner is white, Irish and English from way back. She grew up in Maine, and I wouldn't say we share many similarities, and that's one reason I love her.

VKN: It has been so challenging. Despite being drawn to men sexually, I am not interested in men sexually.

LT: Haha. Yeah, I find gay male porn the most interesting.

VKN: Me too! Why is it the most interesting?

LT: Yes! For me, porn is polarizing. It exists and most of it is misogynistic and created for the biggest porn audience (straight white men or just *men*). For me, I don't get turned on watching someone ram into a woman. I also don't appreciate some lesbian porn because it is so clearly not created for queer people. Women with long painted fingernails . . . Not my thing. On the other hand, I've never watched inclusive queer porn. But the reason I find gay male porn interesting has more to do with: 1) You can obviously tell if someone is turned on. 2) Even if there's pain, it's real and visceral. Whereas, I feel like women have been trained to endure pain. And 3) It's just far removed from my reality, therefore "fantasy."

VKN: What is your "ideal" kind of porn for female? If you could paint that ideal in words.

LT: This is going in a funny direction.

I don't think I can say what the ideal kind of porn is for a female. That's hugely personal, and everyone has different fantasies and different access to material that can turn them on.

VKN: Not where I thought this interview was heading, but I am open to it. This is the first interview in which I feel porn is specifically addressed and I am really glad! I think I have always been afraid to converse about it in an interview because I think society may not make it easy to speak about it without feeling overtly modest or prudish.

LT: I guess you just need the right context and the right audience and maybe the right interviewee.

VKN: I agree! Not a great segue, but can you talk more about your mom? Where did she grow up in Vietnam? And, what does she do?

LT: She grew up in South Vietnam. Long An, maybe less than an hour away from Saigon. She currently owns and operates two different hotels in two different states. My dad was an importer/exporter in Vietnam, and he was born in 1932? He grew up in the North, and quite poor. But rags to riches. By the 1970s, he was one of the richest men in Vietnam (presumably from importing/exporting weapons for the war). My mom met him in her teens and worked for him. I imagine by 1975, they had a more than cordial relationship. My dad was non-monogamous and had many children with many different women. My mom was the last one. My dad fled Vietnam during the fall, and transported people eventually to the United States. The story goes that he fled Vietnam with nothing but two suitcases of gold. Eventually, he started buying and operating hotels in New York, but in a slumlord way. When my dad died, my mom, with little experience doing anything else, followed in those footsteps.

VKN: How was your visit back to Vietnam? Where did you go and what did you see? Do you have a favorite Vietnamese dish? What kind of restaurant, foodwise, do you manage?

LT: I've been to Vietnam twice. Both times for about three weeks. The first trip was a quarter-life crisis trip. I'd been working in a food service job that I felt stagnant at, and on a whim, I bought tickets for under $800 and went by myself. I did what most young tourists do and stayed at hostels and made my way north and around and back south. It was a very lonely but important experience. I felt diasporic more and more. The difference between Vietnamese natives staring at a tall white man and then finding me to stare at was particularly alienating. You don't know what I look like, so I will describe to you. I am 5′ 3″ but strongish, definitely not thin and a little overweight. I felt frustrated in Vietnam as some would mistake me as a man. But I came to peace with it when I was on a flight from Hanoi to HCMC and a woman was struggling to get her suitcase in the overhead compartment, and a Vietnamese man next to her couldn't really assist, but I was taller and bigger and easily threw the luggage up there. It's that moment when I know that I present in a specific way, and it's frustrating being misread all of the time, but understandably so when you just take a straight look at it. (Pun intentional.) But my biggest delight was when I was in Hanoi and there was a fucking gay concert event. It was very baby gay and rainbows, but I had never seen visible Vietnamese queers in such a large context ever, not even in the US.

My favorite Vietnamese dish is probably a toss-up. I love Bún bò Huế. But I also really love Bánh giò, which is very rare to find around.

I part-own a Chinese food restaurant in Portland. It's called XLB after xiao long bao, Chinese soup dumplings. I operate it with my b. partner Jasper. We worked together at a fine dining restaurant called Aviary. Jasper owned that restaurant with his wife and another partner Sarah who was the chef. I quit after a year and a half of cooking, and Jasper quit probably a year or so after. We were friends and stayed in touch, I would help him with some small events, and we conceptually would talk about opening up a chinese food spot. He lived in NYC for about eight years, and I grew up there, and it made sense that we really wanted to have a spot where you could just have good Chinese food.

VKN: My sister just made Bún Bò Huế last Thanksgiving. What is it about Bún Bò Huế that you love? I don't know the Vietnamese queer communities outside of the United States except through YouTube videos—especially this one wedding in Berlin (https://www.youtube.com/watch?v=lXz58aF8jy4)—if you can call a wedding a community, so I am definitely jealous of your baby queer event in Hanoi. Are Vietnamese queers in Vietnam significantly different than the ones in the States?

LT: Definitely. Imagine Vietnam basically experiencing something similar to what the United States felt during the '60s and '70s in terms of a sexual revolution. Now, I have no idea what the sex lives are like of the Vietnamese. But I am thinking more about how the traditional family concept is dissolving. More and more kids in Vietnam are going to college after school instead of setting up families and continuing to support their extended family. It's a more independent way of living, I think (and this is really just me theorizing), that is being mirrored to them through their access to social media and what people in the US and other countries are moving toward as well.

Also, what is that wedding?! That's real money. Where are their parents?! I'm sending this to my family group text and seeing if my mom says anything.

VKN: My cousin who lives in Vietnam who is gay tells me that Vietnamese queer women in Vietnam act like straight guys, misogynistically treating women poorly, emulating their poor, misogynistic counterparts. Is this true? I was so shocked when I saw that fancy-ass wedding. I was like, what the fuck? I have no idea. I just thought: they couldn't be Vietnamese because their wedding was too manicured, Westernly, and it excited me so much! I thought about sending it to my mother, at one point! In terms of Vietnamese couples, I saw this, and it opened my eyes that perhaps Vietnam is really changing? Perhaps?

LT: Have you seen that woman, who is like basically Adam Levine but a Vietnamese woman, on a show that's like *The Voice*? Or that whole *Bachelor* episode in Vietnam? Also, when I travel in Vietnam, I'm still an outsider and very much a tourist, so I've never had access to queer people in Vietnam. I imagine it's a coded world anyway. But isn't it interesting how there must be a butch and there must be a femme?

I think that's absolutely true, but it's a societal problem that is probably true of the whole country. Do the Vietnamese treat women equally? Hell no. Why would we expect same-sex relationships to do the same when we uphold strict power dynamics in relationships?

VKN: I have read about and seen clips from the *Bachelor* episode, about a Viet girl choosing a fellow Viet contestant over the bachelor, but not the Adam Levine Viet girl.

LT: She's not really the Adam Levine Viet Girl, she just happens to probably be queer and a singer and the host of a music contest TV show. Sorry, my exaggeration. Wow, how are you finding all of these YouTube videos?!

VKN: I also watched this one from Canada by Monica Nguyen (https://www.youtube.com/watch?v=-YrgWfhFHKo) and I really love it because it opens an exciting dialogue for other lesbian Vietnamese women—the new millennials. I was doing research because I thought the films I had been watching were either not sapphically fluent or the tenderness was so terrible. I wanted to write a really good script where lesbians knew how to court each other in a postmodern traditional fashion, tenderly and "expertly"—if there is such a thing as contemporary-opulent-sapphic-courting-connoisseurship like Juliet Juliet.

LT: Hm. Are you writing a screenplay?

VKN: I am trying to . . . I am limited by YouTube, but maybe not by my imagination. I am a good erotic writer, when I put my mind to it. How did you court Catie? What was your courtship with her like?

LT: Funnily enough, I would say that she courted me. I think for most of my adult life, I've been seen as a very forward, very direct, confident person. I agree with that for the most part. But I am also the person who would hang out with someone for eight hours, and still have no idea if they're interested in me. With Catie, she presents as a femme, and I'd met her a couple of times and was attracted to her. But treading carefully, I didn't know she was queer until my close friend who lived with her at the time spilled the beans. She was dating another femme-ish person at the time. And I was trying to court someone else when we were both at this Halloween party. But then there was the trip to Vietnam, and then I came back, and she was still living at my friend's house, so I strategically planted myself at their house during the Snowpocalypse of 2017, where I slept on their couch for two nights. Catie was aloof but apparently really into me, and I was nervous because another friend had revealed their crush on me, but it was a conflict because I was interested in Catie and didn't know how to communicate, and it was really Catie who pushed through there.

VKN: I shouldn't have made that assumption. That is a lot of diplomatic, romantic flexing there. How did Catie push through? Are you able to describe? Did she seduce you, ultimately, with her poetry? What kind of poetry does she write? Have you dated a Vietnamese woman? I really love the Vietnamese word(s) for lesbian(s): đồng tính luyến ái nữ—doesn't it look and sound so, so, so, so sexy? Sometimes I think English can be a really crass language for intimacy. I mean they say "love" for pizzas! I don't think I could ever đồng tính luyến ái nữ a pizza!

LT: My mom has only started saying "I love you" this year. It's 2019. I've been alive for twenty-nine years, and it's still a struggle for her. Not that I've ever doubted her love for me, but using the words has been the hardest for her. And I think for me too, but there definitely was a time in eighth grade where I punched people to tell them I liked them.

Oh, *for sure*. The night we opened the restaurant, she texted me to wish me luck. I told her she should come in, that she could be a VIP. She came in with a poem by Chika Sagawa printed on gold tin paper: "I crack an egg and the moon comes out." We also joked that she should write the fortune cookies for the restaurant. Her first fortune: "Yes."

She writes a lot of different poetry; she uses a lot of different mediums as well. I don't know how I'd describe her poetry. It's not explicitly personal, but it's obviously personal. She's telling me that it's "soft-surreal with a touch of sentimentality and engages with nature imagery." That's real!

I have not dated a Vietnamese person. They are obviously hard to come by.

Also, I have never ever looked up the Vietnamese word for lesbian! How unbelievable. I feel really disconnected in a way, partially, because I think Vietnamese culture tried to erase us, tell us that we are merely just friends.

My oldest sister identifies as a lesbian. She's ten years older than me. When I came out at nineteen, my mom called her and yelled at her, told her it was her fault I was gay. My sister got married a few years ago (sadly just got divorced), but the marriage was secret, and Jo was actively a part of our family for that time, but always in an underlying way where we acknowledged and accepted their relationship but would tiptoe around my mother. Now, my mom isn't dumb, but I think for a long time, we kind of had a "don't ask, don't tell" policy. Still do, in some ways.

VKN: Aw! I agree. They are very hard to come by. No worries. I had to translate at one point, so I decided it was important to know its technical terminology. That must sadden you! I would be sad too. Oh, no! So there are a higher population of queer women in your family! Your mother must be so compellingly strong.

LT: Exactly. And I would hate for my mom to think it's "her fault" because she's a strong woman, but in a way, I'd love for my mom to realize how much better off we are in this context. I will never be subjected to the stupid misogyny of a man. I will always know my worth and my power and it's a strength my mom taught us.

VKN: The rest of your siblings are brothers, yes? Or are there more sisters?

LT: Four sisters and a brother. My mom struggled with a few miscarriages, but she had all of us three years apart, except for my brother, who is one year older than me.

VKN: I hope your brother is a lesbian!

LT: My brother is very straight, very attracted to women, but damn, he sometimes is more queer than I am!

VKN: So he is a lesbian after all. He is into women! Why do you think he is sometimes more queer than you are?

LT: I think he really understands his identity in the context of the world. He is a Vietnamese man, a millennial, and really a star. I think he lives understanding the blurriness of how the world was built and how we can actually dismantle it using new tools. That's a weird way to describe him, but he got a new job recently, and his title is "Director of Innovation." And he is that, for sure. I think he is comfortable with his sexuality and isn't afraid of what people think of him. That's pretty queer.

VKN: You must be so proud of him! DOI! Which means life (đời) in Vietnamese. We have covered so much autobiographical and queer real estate here, Laura. Thank you for being so open with me!

LT: My brother is sweet, but very complicated, and I am proud of him, but in some ways saddened by our weird relationship. But that's siblings for you. We definitely need work in the communication bit. Love him though.

APPLES AND PEARS

Sophia Lee

I was twelve when I took a pair of rusty scissors to my hair: long hair grown out over the course of a decade lay mangled on the bathroom floor. It was a murder scene, complete with the killer—me; the murder weapon—my old, dirty scissors; and the victim—my mother. In a mixture of blind rage and grief, she snatched the scissors out of my shaking hands and screamed,   "*Why?*"

It's been seven years and I still don't know what made her angrier, the mess or me.

And it's funny, the way the roles have reversed. There was no anger when my sisters and I sat patiently in the very same bathroom years earlier, my mother circling around us, eyeing errant strands she deemed "too long" for summer heat. My mother cutting our hair in perfect imitation of the bowls we ate out of because that's the way it should be. Apples and pears, peeled and quartered, on the countertop for later.

But now she's screaming, and she won't stop. She won't stop going on about the man in me, the one she sees at every passing glance, in every conversation where the start and end are always bleak: always a reminder that masculinity is *ugly* . . . in a woman. A good, honest woman should be quiet, small. She should be smart but not witty. She should wear dresses and heels and her hair should always be pristine: up, down, in braids, or plain, but never shorter than the distance from the top of her head to the tops of her ears. A woman with short hair. What a queer thing to be.

But it's not just Mom. She only reads from pamphlets. It's all the boys and the girls and the preachers in the church we go to in Queens. Every Sunday is a reminder to keep in line. We eat cup after cup of microwavable instant noodles, hissing at the way it burns our tongues, sucking at the stains on our teeth. Meanwhile, the preacher warns of the perils of gluttony. We show off the new DS games we bought with our parents' money, tell each other how much better we are at them than anyone else ever could be. The preacher sermons about the perils of excess pride. The boys talk about X-rated movies and the girls pretend to be disgusted, throwing looks over their shoulders to make sure their parents don't suspect a thing. The preacher rails against sins of intimacy: adultery, early pregnancy.

Deviancy.

Everyone nods their heads in an unwavering show of faith. My mother looks at me, for the first time in hours, making sure I've heard every word. Every Sunday, like clockwork, time suspends for long enough to make me feel untethered. And then, it's over. The kids keep talking about their X-rated dreams. The preacher drones on about the futility of religious disbelief. My mom and I don't look at each other for the rest of Sunday.

It's Sunday again, but we're not at church. I'm standing in our bathroom, chunks of my own hair gripped anxiously in my hands as my mother screams at me to be normal. I look at myself in the mirror and it's jarring. It's scary and new and I'm not sure what to do with my hands. My eyes shift away from my reflection and I see her. I see her, glaring over my shoulder, right where dark, black curtains used to block her from view. We meet eyes and for the first time in years, I remember what I used to know very well; every Sunday, like clockwork, time suspends.

She begs me to be normal.

I say I finally am.

I don't check to make sure she's heard.

BIRD'S VIEW

Chen Xiangyun/谌翔云

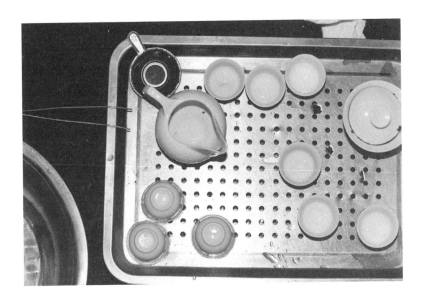

FOUNDATION

Chen Xiangyun/谌翔云

SOUTH OF THE RIVER

Chen Xiangyun/谌翔云

YAY

Chen Xiangyun/谌翔云

MARY POPPINS

Chen Xiangyun/谌翔云

HAIRMELON

Chen Xiangyun/谌翔云

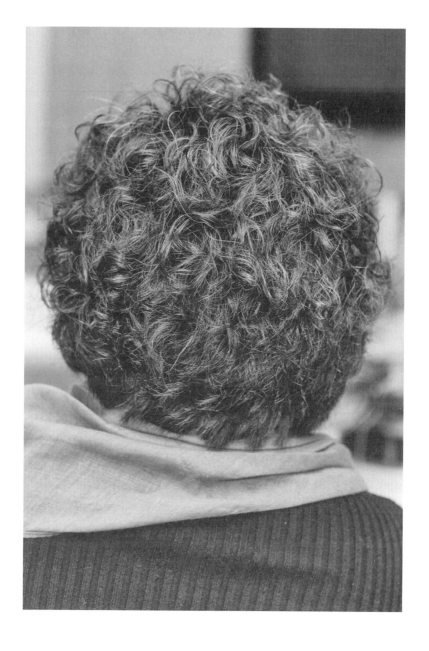

OLIVIA AND CHEN ZHAN

Chen Xiangyun/谌翔云

THAT'S RIGHT

Chen Xiangyun/谌翔云

ABBY, OLIVIA AND DAD

Chen Xiangyun/谌翔云

T-SET

Chen Xiangyun/谌翔云

AMA

Chen Xiangyun/谌翔云

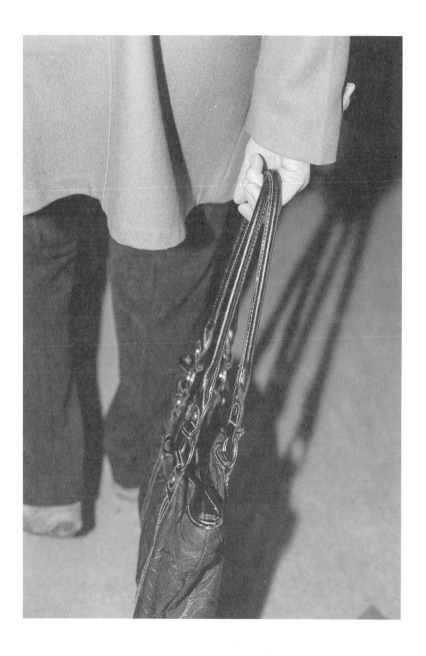

TA CHẠM LÊN NGƯỜI MÌNH YÊU THẾ NÀO?

Uyen T. Phạm

1-. I can let English –penetrate> my Vietnamese,
certain of who I am and what I am saying. But often times,
my Vietnamese refuses to penetrate English.

2-. Bà ngoại's home garden
was where only the eight-year-old me could roam around
and bury treasures.
Tôi lớn lên trong cái mảnh vườn nhỏ đó,
chẳng bao giờ tưởng tượng sẽ có ai khác ở ngoài vào
grow her vegetables,
eat her fruits,
touch her **đất**.

3-. Tôi có một đứa bạn là người Mỹ gốc Việt,
người tôi gọi bằng tên đệm là My khi kể chuyện với mẹ.
In her mind, there's no Paige.

4-. Có lần tôi vào hiệu sách,
tình cờ tìm thấy một quyển dạy tiếng Việt cho người nước ngoài
mà đứng cùng con bạn cười sặc sụa
vì văn chương trong đó nghe quá giả tạo.
Quả nhiên:
Phong ba bão táp không bằng ngữ pháp Việt Nam.

5-. Tôi yêu thứ ngôn ngữ khó chiều này,
this monogamy.

6-. My people would readily applaud a dude's Xin chào in
his white accent.

7-. Tôi chỉ dùng tiếng Việt ở đây when I need to explain something, a term in my language that's impossible to be replaced. My translation policy has always been about being under -stood.

8-. Nỗi sợ của việc họ không hiểu tôi nói gì lớn hơn nỗi sợ rằng tôi không thể nói tiếng Việt. (Is this survivor mode?)

9-. Lớn lên, tôi luôn được dạy phải khiêm tốn. Ừ thì vì thế mà bọn Châu Á được coi là model minority đấy. Bố tôi bảo rằng ra nước ngoài thì phải quen và hòa nhập được với lối sống của họ mới là giỏi. "Hòa nhập," một từ nghe rất tích cực trong tiếng Việt nhưng dịch ra tiếng Anh lại rất triggering: integrate, assimilate.

10-. Không biết assimilate đến mức nào thì humility biến thành humiliation?

11-. Tôi chẳng bao giờ xấu hổ với việc là người Việt, nhưng cũng chưa từng cố gắng khiến ai ở đây tin vào điều đó.

12-. Khi nói tiếng Anh, tôi thường phải trở thành một con người khác. And when I speak Vietnamese, well. I'm just me. Có lẽ vấn đề nằm ở đó. Tôi sợ những người ở đây không chấp nhận việc tôi chỉ là bản
thân mình,
tôi luôn phải là hơn thế, until I'm more than myself

but not fully myself,
another self.
Phần bị mất đi đó, tôi vẫn chẳng rõ thiếu điều ấy
thì tôi còn là mình nữa không.

13-. Tiếng Việt hay ngồi khiêm tốn và lặng lẽ trong góc phòng
watch English and me kiss.
When I vomit, she washes my mouth.

14.- To love her: chỉ mình tôi là đủ,
tôi có thể lần trong da thịt mình thứ tình yêu ấy.
To love him: tôi luôn phải đi mượn, đi vay,
những sự vay mượn không biết tìm đâu trả (lại).

15-. Những lúc tuyệt vọng nhất, tôi nói chuyện với mình bằng
tiếng Việt.

16.-.Tôi lắng nghe tiếng mình thở. Tiếng cô ấy th   ở. Tiếng cậu ta t
h   ở.

ON THESE STREETS, EVERY QUEER WOMAN IS ROADKILL

S.E. *Swea*

No amount of air-conditioning can keep me
in a car too long, my body repels the static,
it has never known a standard of rest still enough
to pass for something ladylike. I would always
rather walk, even in this heat, even on these streets,
walk till my soles blister and then walk some more yet
until there is enough distance cleared between me
and my final destination to cut myself a little loose.
It's thirty degrees today, no clouds in the sky for miles
and miles. Thirty degrees and still steadily going, going, the sun a spot so bright it burns me out
of my own skin, shrivels me into a carcass so condensed
all it would take is a lighter to set me to smoke.
I often dream of fire and brimstone. No matter how
far I run, the sermons follow, a crawling cruise behind
my stumble but fast enough to keep me in sights, to
flash me a warning light as it crushes someone less lucky
under its wheels and backs up just to run over them again.
They were found, I was told, in their car, doing what
girls in love do. I wonder what they must have done
when the men first came. I wonder what it would take
to break a person so much, they would apologise for
being hurt. I wonder, if they were on foot like me,
would they have gotten away? And more importantly,
would they have wanted to?
If it were me I would have run. Run from the rotan,
its swishes and cracks against soft skin, run from
the weight of a crowd's oppressive stare, run from
that state, this country, as far as I could for as long

as I could. But it was not me they found in the car,
even if it was me that cried for them. In this body
no stamina, however impressive, can carry me as far
as that. In this body I am not as strong as them, to stand
when my name is called, to stay, to endure. I wonder
if most of my anxiety is not just rehearsal for a day
when it will be me caught under those spoked wheels,
when I sink into the molten street gasping for breath.
I wonder if the only oasis in this country is a reflection
of a woman's face, and if the bodies by the roadside
aren't just landmarks of men's violence.
In truth, I am not really running. I don't think any of
us can. Not the lesbians in Terengganu, Nur Sajat and
her children, Nisha Ayub and her portrait, nor all the
gay and trans women found daily dead-
named and written out of our own histories. Not
the women who have heard so many iterations of venom
they have turned it into a language, inward and outward
till our fangs are flashing toward any predator that
rolls our way. And maybe if you walk long enough,
far enough, you just might shake the dogs behind you.
Maybe you might slip through the interstate unseen,
board a plane bound westward, make your daring getaway.
But even standing here in this body, I feel too tired for that,
and the heat is sapping what life left in my legs till
I feel like nothing but a husk of myself, charred meat.
Here is the baton, then, run for me like I ran for them.
If nothing else, I pray you have the strength to turn and
face your pursuers at the finish-line, spit every name that
built you from the sole up and watch it drip off their faces.
Honour every sister before you, all us wretched roadkill.

THE PHYSIOLOGY OF A FAKE ASIAN

Kaye Lin Kuphal

开端 (kāi duān) [inception]
Bodies are anatomically aqueous,
controlled in bulk
by hydrogen bonds:
stabilizing, secretive, circulative, shapechanging but estranged
inside skin.
Bringing balance, the soul speaks both water and bone.
At my soul's incipience, the progenitors of my possibility had
intercourse
(consensual or rape? Did mother know father?),
and I became an ethnically Chinese woman
(yellow skin, silky straight dark hair, upper eyelids thicker than
Caucasians')
with gigantism localized to my left foot.

被抛弃 (bèi pāo qì) [to be abandoned]
During the one-child policy of China, my birth mother
abandoned me.
Surgery was expensive, my disability might have kept me
from polishing the backbones of the dragon,
as the Guilin terraces are called,
and the fee for another child was sometimes a year's income.
Those aside, daughters marry into husband's families whereas
sons stay,
lending to a desire to have sons to carry on the family name
and take care of the parents.
The misogyny is so dense
that it becomes cultural practice.
At an orphanage, I was named
千千 (Qiān Qiān) [Thousand Thousand].

领养 (lǐng yǎng) [adoption]
I was adopted and renamed Kaye Lin for my Mandarin name
(like the metric prefix) and my birthplace. On January 12, 1999,
my German-American parents brought me to Kentucky.
A podiatric surgeon operated on me. I gained no weight
during my first year of adoption.

更迭 (gēng dié) [alternation]
Sometimes I imagine
what if I had been left in China.
Everyone else is moving like the Big Ones do, but I can't,
I hurt. Who is leaving?
Big One tells me not to cry,
Mamas and Dadas are coming.
Where are mine?

背景 (bèi jǐng) [setting]
The late nineties,
what a time to be Chinese in the US.
A little white girl shouted "Mulan!" at me, excited to see a
Chinese hero.
My friend Hayley, another adopted Chinese-American, believes
the film inspired
her sister Camille's adoption.
We were a China doll set
pushed along the white river rushing through Kentucky living.

青春 (qīng chūn) [adolescence]
I liked being good at math-music-grades as others expected.
To be closer to my crush, Mary, which muddled me
since Confirmation said gayness was wrong,
I joined band. My lungs learned vibrato
and the joy of shimmering air with sound.
The body is used well when making music.

I also hated myself for fulfilling expectations
and for my quietness being taken as an inability with English.
Someone asked if I was a foreign exchange student,
and I had lived in Owensboro longer than she had.
For peace, I caused myself pain, knifed through webbings
between fingers and toes, was it pencil-pen-stone scratching
skin off wrist?
My watch bands smelled like rancid blood.
Angry-sad-numb-confused-in terror—
pain helped. I am addicted to the endorphins released
when I batter my body.
I love and despise it.

更迭 (gēng dié) [alternation]
I talk to the girl I like. A boy comes up, says it's not normal,
it must be Western. He lands a fist. I stay down.
If people want to be my parents, hasten,
give me someplace to be other than here.

燃烧 (rán shāo) [to burn]
"Homosexuals will burn in a lake of fire!" a boy declared.
A teacher continued, "Homosexuality is like bestiality.
They shouldn't act on their urges. I could go and shove girls
against lockers, but I don't." I was silent.
You never get over being told to burn.

更迭 (gēng dié) [alternation]
I think of cutting myself and instead sleep for work. The boss likes
my good fingers if not feet. I need a cheap cane
to keep at this damned life.

现实 (xiàn shí) [reality]
At my college, Colgate University, a Republican group mocked
those certain to suffer under Trump presidency.

Their chats were publicized:
"So just because somebody is a different race than me we
should make their
voices more important? Sounds like the 3/5ths compromise
but in reverse."
"Let them cry. We won. They will get over it soon enough."
"This week I have made a girl cry and denied white privilege
in class."
A white cisgender gay member was involved. When queer
people of color asked
white queer people to address how they increase racism, they
refused.
Racism, colorism, and anti-blackness matter.
Media raises queer people of color to believe that gayness is
for white people,
and white queers perform the worst betrayals.

自暴自弃 (zì bào zì qì) [to abandon oneself to despair]
I wrote down all the death-desire, and my boss sent the police
to my home, my Ama's home.
I had to get them out, for my family was brown,
and they were armed and white. They took me in handcuffs
to the hospital when I said no to a psychologist coming to me.
My mental health was never supposed to take over
my family home like that, like aggression and demand and disdain
for the criminal activity of being trapped and tricked by my
own mind.
I feared my lack of insurance and my hospital room,
bare except for my body atop the bed, restraints hanging off
the sides.
Somehow I talked my way out of staying in that psych ward,
the instinct to avoid being potentially assaulted there
taking over my stunned self into speaking as if a normal person.
Since then, I have been having panic attack after cry after panic
attack

after more of the same depression common to my existence.
I always had a name for how the darkness takes me over.
Now, I know I cannot let others know how well I know that
                                                named thing,
for I simply cannot be back there again.
I fear it more than outright death.

继续前行 (jì xù qián xíng) [continuing going forward]
Sometimes I wish my birth mother had left me not to be found,
but to die. I must learn that I really can be Chinese-American
                                                and lesbian.
Will my water overwhelm my bone
or my bone hold its place firmly at last?
The shapechange continues, keeping my interest.

IN CONVERSATION WITH VI KHI NAO
Kaye Lin Kuphal

VI KHI NAO: What inspires you to write "The Physiology of a Fake Asian?" I found the title insightful and catchy. And, how did you arrive to such a bold and comedic title?

KAYE LIN KUPHAL: It started out as a prose memoir for class, and I wanted to honor all sorts of parts of myself, the scientific part of me and the part of me that feels to be at a peculiar liminal space in the Chinese American community. I find, at times, it can be fairly absurd to navigate, thus the sort of playful title.

VKN: Why is it absurd to navigate?

KLK: There are various cultural aspects that I do not have the strongest ties to. I took Saturday Chinese classes for a while, as one does, but having grown up in an area with an extremely small Asian community, as I moved and made my way to other communities, I felt and often still feel as if a sort of imposter while also being aware of the complicated politics of how I arrived here and why I know what I know.

VKN: Are you fluent in Mandarin? How do you feel about your orphanage name? 千千 (Qiān Qiān) [Thousand Thousand]. Did you ever want to be Hundred Hundred? What is an ideal name for you—if you were to name yourself? When I think of Thousand Thousand, I think of origami and cranes and dreams coming true from persistency.

KLK: I am not fluent in Mandarin, so I constantly ask other people this or that question as I fumble about what I originally babbled in. I think I mostly enjoy how I went from one Thousand to another Thousand since numbers are all kinds of fun. I think I am already fairly attached to my name. It has served me well, and I love seeing the face of my friends as I explain how my adoptive parents arrived at my renaming.

VKN: Can you talk more about Owensboro? What it is like to grow up there? And, when did you know that you are a lesbian? Did you come out immediately or did you take your time? What was your first Sapphic experience like? You are engaged, yes? When will you get married? Our interview takes place during Pride Month. Do you feel prideful? And, where in the world are you? Is it accepting where you are at?

KLK: Owensboro is a small city in Kentucky, and hopefully there is still a small Asian market or two the size of a two-bedroom apartment. There is a lot of variance within it, people who see KKK recruitment materials around them and people who simply see their lawns and farms and people who want desperately to leave or never leave. I knew I was a lesbian in my early teenage years, and coming out was the process of many years of feeling out others' receptiveness. I had a crush on a girl who, when I eventually confessed to her, called it all an abomination, so that was what it was, but I wrote some fantastically silly things along that way. I am engaged indeed, and we are waiting to set a date; living in Hawai'i, destination tourism does a lot to the pockets and community's economy. I feel a reasonable amount of pride, I suppose, as far as moving away from the South and the way people look at me and my partner when we are about, being more used to the way I move through the world, and finally being somewhere where it is decently okay to be both Asian and lesbian, although the journey will certainly continue onward.

VKN: I love how translucent and lucid your memoristic poem "The Physiology of a Fake Asian" is. How you are able to cover so much psychic, linguistic, political, emotional space within one lyrical space, even if that space has been fashioned into twelve movements. Did you see the shape of the poem before you produced it or did the form arrive to you as you were unraveling?

KLK: The poem has another form in this ungodly mass of prose, so shaping it down seemed the thing to do to make it get to the needed spaces in a more visible and approachable way. Editing from that desire, I arrived at this form.

VKN: What other form is that, Kaye? You described it as "ungodly mass of prose"—Like a gigantic block of prose that went on forever? Or just pages and pages of prose that may be or may not be chaotic? I am trying to imagine the birth of its origin. Like a star being born.

KLK: I suppose a bit of both, details upon details of my life, tangents into friends' lives, and trying to make sense of the memories I have as they attempt to escape my consciousness.

VKN: What part of this poem was the most difficult to write? Did it take you long to produce it?

KLK: I think the Mandarin subheadings and then reforming accordingly took the most effort and time. There was a lot of reaching out about one of the things I feel somewhere between insecure and disappointed about—the language I lost coming here—but it was mostly an emotional aspect in difficulty since in measured time, it came about reasonably.

VKN: I am particularly drawn to this stanza: "Will my water overwhelm my bone / or my bone hold its place firmly at last?" It's more abstract than your other lines. Can you talk more about the source or logic behind these two lines?

KLK: Knowing myself to be within my body is a difficulty of mine. Call it dissociation, or the like. When I consider myself, I view myself as being solid and liquid in confusion, kind of like glass, seeking to settle but by nature in some transition behavior.

VKN: Your poem addresses the following concern, "Media raises queer people of color to believe that gayness is for white people, / and white queers perform the worst betrayals." Based on such specious premise, what kind of visibility do you desire for Asian sapphicity? Or for yourself? Where in the landscape of ethnic gayness do you wish to belong? And, what do you think those two lines mean?

KLK: I would love for Asian sapphicity to in general be more societally prominent, and accordingly help broaden perceptions on who Asians and queer people are, particularly surrounding predations and attacks on them. I would also love to see more interaction with other communities of color and internationally, as far as matters dealing with urban, rural, homeland versus wherever "here" is, all the history and physicality we move through. I think I would just like to belong anywhere I feel there are good communication and unspoken truths, but these are difficult—I love the relationships I have with other queer people of color, and I think the lines of being Asian and being lesbian have threads in how my partner and I have had our own and then joined journeys in coming out, coming to this home, really delving into these essential aspects of ourselves and having pride in how we are seen and how we love each other and the family and friends around us.

VKN: Why are they difficult, Kaye?

KLK: There are a lot of fraught, complicated things as far as inter-Asian politics, antiblackness, racism with their contextual breadths and depths depending on the communities moved through. I guess a particular moment is when the Trump travel ban came out, and I received a call from my partner about our Ama being frantic because she was worried about not being able to see her family in the Philippines again if it spread to that degree. She is there now, luckily, but when things of that matter happen, being hyperaware of who around you cares at all and understands the effect of such policies tends toward poignancy.

VKN: Are you a full-time writer/poet? Or do you exist in other disciplines, workwise? Does your literary life intersect with your livelihood? Is there a book that you highly recommend? Are you working on a book? Or do you prefer only one poem to exist in the world and it's enough? What is your literary ambition like?

KLK: Workwise, I am simply working retail for my livelihood as I feel out my existence in other disciplines. I love what I got my degree in, biochemistry, but the world of lab research is decently competitive, and I have a lot of things I want to give myself to writing. I do not think there is a lot of intersection currently, but I would love to have more integration of my interests. For example, one of the writing projects I have yet to really get into is a sort of a new Magic School Bus series, playing around with altered physical laws and getting to see many, many children on the page and the consequences of weird science. As far as books I recommend, *Not Here* by Hieu Minh Nguyen. I am working on a manuscript, which I hope becomes something full and rich. I suppose my ambition is both vast and patient as I would like to see a lot of ideas through, and while excited about working toward their realization, I do not feel rushed about getting them together.

VKN: Would you like your adopted parents to read this poem? What kind of responses do you desire from the world? Do you wish to connect more with the Asian Lesbian community? Or would you like to be quietly or privately or psychically connected without much social engagements?

KLK: There is a part of me that hopes they do and another part that does not mind. I have always been rather insular aside from when I have thought and written enough to say things in writing publicly. I would like for fellow Asian adoptees to feel more connected, to find more ways to interact with Asian lesbians, to take this life and make more generally positive connections.

VKN: Reeds, instruments, selfies, dog, fiancé, etc., the high-lights of your Instagramic life: In one of your Instagram posts, there are several pictures of a dog. Is that your dog? What is your dog like/named?

KLK: Ah, I think that is my parents' dog. She is pretty playful and attached, Cinny is. When I visit my parents' home, sometimes I will fall asleep with her lying full on top of me, and that is a lovely moment.

VKN: Can you talk about your love for reeds? Are they your favorite/preferred instruments to play? When did you develop your love for them? What do they sound like? Are they simi-lar to your writing? If not, is it a different expression of your cre-ativity? I have heard you play the piano on your Instagram, which sounded methodical and peaceful to me. There was an element of unspoken sadness about it too.

KLK: I love the meticulousness of playing a double reed instrument and having to know all these techniques to make the mouthpiece, the reed, work. From gouging cane to tying up a blank to sharpening and shaping and shaping and sharpening, it is rhythmic and interesting, and while they sound horrible, like a mad duck's call, just before they are performance quality, it still amazes me how to get to make music. I think they are a different expression of my creativity as I do one or the other more in a way that follows my mood and how I want to connect with myself and others. Musically and literarily, I tend to feel as if I am in B or D minor in six-eight time.

VKN: I like to ask food questions because I really love cooking. Is there a dish you can't live without?

KLK: I love a bowl of jasmine rice with a bit of oil and salt, wonderful accompaniment for almost anything, including my incessant desire for pork and chive dumplings.

ORACLE DECK

Jessica Jiang

COWHERD & WEAVER GIRL
牛郎织女 　天

Spirits sing of a young cowherd and her forbidden lover who weaves the clouds, reunited in the heavens once a year by a bridge of magpies. On the seventh day of the seventh month you may redeem this card to win the temporary favor of the gods, or to travel great distances to a place your heart desires.

For one turn:
+3 Animal handling
+2 Religion

LEFT-BEHIND WIFE
番客婶 　阴

In this village full of women, money comes from across the ocean - remittances from a place called Gold Mountain. You'll likely never see your husband again, but maybe your sons will when they grow up. Still, this life is far from lonely.

If you play this character, you gain +100 yuan every other turn but gain +1 suspicion from your mother-in-law every time you meet your lover.

SWORN SISTERS
老同 　花

The stars foretold your perfect pairing before either of you left your mothers' wombs. What a stroke of fate to end up sworn sisters, rather than husband and wife. Some secrets can only be shared between women, in a script illegible to men.

Language proficiency: 女书 (Nüshu)
+1 Performance
+2 Arcana

DIASPORA LESBIAN
华侨拉拉 　阳

"Maybe if we had raised you in China, things would have been different," your mother says in the car. You say nothing because you know better. Your history is butch Asian dykes at Christopher Street Liberation Day but also 自梳女 a century ago in Guangdong and all the other wayward girls who refused to marry men.

+3 History
+2 Stealth

DYKES

K-Ming Chang

When they rebuild Las Vegas into a replica of Venice, complete with chlorinated canals and waterfront bakeries that sell bread in the shape of breasts, they find where Ail's house detached from the ground, dragging entrails of light behind it. The shadow of the house remains, but they can't find what is casting it. The shadow, dense as the moles on Ail's neck, can always be seen on the street, even when there isn't a sun to sew its shape on the ground. They think at first that the shadow is some kind of stain, but when they stand a skyscraper in the same spot, the shadow is still the size of Ail's old house. The shape of her house is as permanent to me as my own name: its roof crumpled like a handkerchief, its walls the color of ham, the fence pulled out like teeth. She once grew a wall of shrubs and pissed on them at night, which was the only way to water them without getting fined.

Ail was the girl all languages were invented to describe. Her hair was the same color as quiet. She had slit pupils like a cat's, which she claimed were natural, though I once saw her take out contact lenses in the sink, rinsing them twice before her eyes licked them in again. In the bathroom of the restaurant, she braided her hair in ways that hadn't been invented yet: in a noose around her neck, or in two balls that rested above her ears, or in clusters all over her scalp like fish eggs. She wore it in a shower cap when we were working, which made her head resemble the translucent fish eggs we smeared onto the tops of our deluxe California rolls.

Ail's name, unlike her eyes, was real. Her mother misspelled *Ali* on her birth certificate. When we first met, she introduced herself as *three-letter synonym for sickness, guess.* Ail and I worked at a sushi restaurant in New Chinatown Plaza, where we injected red dyes into the raw fish to make the flesh look more edible. Our boss confused the words *edible* and *flammable,* and Ail once joked about spraying the fish with propane instead. Our boss was a man from Hong Kong who only drank water after he'd boiled it twice because water in the desert—so he claimed—was actually purified piss from sewage pipes. One week, rain tore up the seams of the sky and he lined the sidewalk with buckets, telling us to start selling rainwater for twice the price of bottled water.

When I asked Ail why the fish had to be redder, she told me that's what Vegas is all about: plagiarism. Our fish were plagiarized from the sea. Our bodies were plagiarized from TV. I told her no one would believe the fish was any good anyway because we were so far from the Pacific, far from any body of water wider than a toilet.

Ail laced her apron like a corset. She wore all her clothes like a period costume, except I could never tell what period. When I first got the job standing behind the glass window of the sushi counter, where I said *O-hi-O* to every tourist who walked in, Ail taught me how to crimp the rice and suture the seaweed skin. *Each roll should be about the width of a penis,* she said. She circled her fingers to show me. To make me laugh, she pretended to jack off the sushi every time the customer had his head down, handling his chopsticks as if they were on fire. I watched her hands, slick with rice vinegar and Windex, arranging the rice like lace around slivers of dye-injected fish. Sometimes I injected too much red dye and the fish-flesh turned veiny with blood. When this happened, Ail pinched up the red-ruined fish and folded it into her mouth and swallowed without chewing. She said she was practicing for when she was old and had no teeth, just like her grandmother, the one who still lived next to the Taoyuan International airport and named each airplane as it spent the sky. *You have to give them names,* she'd told Ail over the phone, *or else they won't land.* Ail's grandmother thought that planes were called down. She thought the wings of airplanes were actually giant ears that listened to men on the runway, landing when its name was called down.

What our boss really wanted was to open a Sushi Boat. Not the kind of restaurant where the sushi revolved past you on a conveyor belt, but an actual boat for the customers to board. The Sushi Boat would be a vessel large enough to seat one thousand people, and it would float inside a reservoir where fish lived, freshwater and saltwater breeds coexisting through some aquatic miracle, and the customers could rent fishing poles on the boat and catch their own live fish and we would slaughter and butcher them on an elevated stage. We told our boss this was unrealistic for multiple reasons, the first being that he owned no reservoir, and the second being that he had no boat. Our boss said he was working on both. He'd begun to build a boat in the dumpster-lined lot behind the restaurant, but the boat was the size of one man, and it was assembled from various duct-taped pieces of garbage: cardboard from a TV box, Styrofoam cases that arrived with our phalluses of iced fish, a two-by-four sawed into eight mismatched pieces, and a hull hammered out of a retired wok. It looked more like the ribcage of some strange suburban trash-beast than a thing that could float, but we named it anyway, christening the ship by cracking open a bottle of rice wine against its side. There was a family of raccoons living inside the dented hull, wedged between the cardboard bottom of the boat and the greasy tarp our boss used to cover it. We named the raccoons after our grandmothers, who died in cities we had never seen. The raccoon mother abandoned her children that spring, and there were four raccoon babies in total, curdled inside the boat with their oil-bright fur and their claws soft as cheese. During lunch break, Ail tossed them garbage instead of flinging it into the dumpster, and they ate fists of napkins and bendy straws slicked with lipstick and avocado bits and edamame skins until they grew up, faster than we thought possible, and learned to climb into the dumpster by themselves. After that, we saw them only at the end of our night shifts, and even then we only saw their eyes, so bitter-bright we mistook them for stars, except that they moved too fast to be stars and crowded us out of the dark, those eyes constellating our lives, those eyes clotting and fanning out like flies as the raccoons passed trash to each other. Ail and I watched them feast for hours, their hunger almost a color, until we saw one of the babies—who was no longer a baby but bigger than its mother—begin eating the boat, gnawing down the sail made of someone's apron. The raccoons swarmed into the boat, darning the sides with their teeth, and when the sun began to liquefy the pavement with light, it looked like they were riding out to sea.

Ail's grandmother spoke to her in Japanese. Ail's name on the phone was Akiko, which meant sparkling child, which prompted Ail to buy a perfume with glitter in it. The glitter got onto the fish and the customers loved it, thinking it was some kind of edible glitter to match the Strip and its perpetual light, so Ail began spraying the perfume directly into the rice.

Ail was the one who taught me to say *Ohio*, which meant good morning. I once thought this was because it was always morning in Ohio, but years later, when I kissed a white girl from Ohio in the dark of her car and told her this while I was naked, because it was the kind of thing you could only say to a person when you were naked with them, the girl laughed at me. Her molars glowed like moths and flew at my face.

Ohio, I said to Ail. We said good morning even when it was nighttime and our last shift began, the customers drunk and so hungry they didn't care that Ail was pretending to jack off the sushi. They thought we were Japanese, though the red-gold gate outside said New Chinatown Plaza and my nametag claimed my name was Lee. *As in Bruce*, I told Ail when we first met. She'd been spraying Windex on the sushi mats even though the chemicals were toxic, and when I told her this, she said *what do you care, Bruce? You're already dead.* Ail and I spent our first day discussing Bruce Lee assassination plots: Ail said the FBI had drugged him on set. I said Bruce had flown back to Hong Kong without telling anyone, and that his plane was still in orbit, waiting to land somewhere he didn't have to fight anyone.

Ail told me that in Taiwan, there were old Japanese houses with ghosts inside them. I asked her what the ghosts looked like and she skated her thumbnail across my neck. A necklace of sweat slid down into my shirt. Behind the sushi counter, Ail stood so close that her breath was up my nose. *They're headless ghosts,* she said. She pretended to twist off her head and cleave it open like a melon. The customers clapped, thinking she was doing a Japanese dance. Our boss overheard the applause and said maybe we should do performances too, just like every bar on the Strip. *The people want strippers,* he said. He looked at Ail's breasts, but they were sheathed behind her apron. I imagined she had nipples as broad as my palms. I'd told her this once, and she said I could look if I wanted, but I knew all wants were weapons that could be turned on you anytime. I thought of the story about the woman who turned to salt when she looked back at a city. The moral was either you shouldn't look back or you shouldn't be a woman. I couldn't remember if the woman had been naked or not, but I knew if I looked at Ail too long, her body would slump into a mound of MSG.

Our boss began every sentence with *the people want.* When we asked him why he opened a sushi restaurant in the middle of a desert, he'd said: *The people want sushi. The people don't want MSG.* After that, Ail and I bought a ten-pound bag of MSG from the Ranch 99 across the street and dazzled his tea with pinches of it. We pretended we were poisoning him with it, that he would die a little every day until he was completely ours. Ail said we would butcher his body with our sushi knives, store different pieces of him in different sacks of rice, steal all his money and his BMW, and drive out of the desert like women in love. I'd never heard her use the word *love,* and the word was a wasp in her mouth. I wanted to snag it out of the air with my tongue, neuter its stinger by swallowing it.

That night, when we went home, Ail and I practiced our stripping. She even let me touch her unbraided hair, which had grown all the way to her wrists. She whipped off her protective shower cap and I saw for the first time how pale her scalp was, how much it resembled the seam of fat in the slabs of salmon we sliced to the thickness of our lips. Our boss told us we should come tomorrow wearing shorter skirts. *Sex and food are symmetrical appetites*, he said. *The people want to be fed.* If that were true, Ail said, men would only want to put it in your mouth. In the dark of her one-room apartment, we tried taking off our clothes with our teeth. Her mother had left for a bartending job already, and the moon broke in through the window. The moon was the only man in the room. Ail told me we would look sexy, but in the dark I didn't feel like a body, just a hole eating itself empty. I couldn't tell where my mouth was until Ail opened it with her fingers and tacked my lips back. She said my teeth were a horse's. I told her horses didn't live in the desert unless there was a man riding it, letting it drink from his palms. Ail cupped her hands in the dark, a slur of wrist. I knelt and lowered my head into her hands, my neck a noose of skin. Our bodies moved like they were jointed together, my legs sewn to her torso, my tongue arming her mouth.

When I walked home that night, my father was asleep on the sofa. He made me microwave the sashimi I'd brought back from the restaurant. *I'm Chinese*, he said. *We don't eat things raw.* My mother—before her death—had been born on the same island as Ail's, an island where the military determined everything, even the size of the moon at night, even what language you spoke in the dark and which language you spoke in the light. She'd married my father because she'd been told a long time ago: always fall asleep with a weapon beside you. *Why do we need weapons*, my mother must have thought, *when we have men?*

You should see these mainlanders, my father said, a slab of dyed salmon dangling from his mouth like a tongue. The sashimi was dissolving into soap-foam. *These mainlanders,* he kept saying, as if he wasn't one. He was a dealer in the casinos, and while manning a poker table, one of the players told him that Asians had natural poker faces. *You're so expressionless,* she'd said, *you could win without trying.* My father had said nothing, but later that day I caught him standing in front of the bathroom mirror, prying at his cheeks and lips and chin, pinning them into expressions that were all variations of the same pain.

When Ail and I talked about our fathers, we realized we could be describing the same man. We even began to borrow details from each other's descriptions: *My father is so near-sighted he can't see his own shit when he flushes,* she said. *That's my father,* I said. *Your father got Lasik surgery back when it was still experimental.*

Ail told me that Lasik eye surgery was invented by a Taiwanese man. We began to tell facts about Taiwan to all our customers. When we ran out of facts—Ail had already described the airport twice and the only fact I knew was *my mother was born there*—Ail began to steal facts about China and Japan. *This is called reverse-colonization,* Ail told me. In Japan, she said, strawberries grew fat as teats. They filled syringes with water and injected them into the fruits until they flexed with muscle. When I told her that was lie, she said *let's go to Japan tonight and I'll prove it to you.*

The Strip was an empire made up of every country: that night, we walked to the Eiffel Tower and licked the Leaning Tower of Pisa and took pictures beside the miniature globe that was gooey with light and looked more like a spitball than our planet. We watched the Bellagio fountain show, water spewing up the sky, and looked through the glass revolving doors where the tourists ate choco-late-glazed strawberries from mirrored trays, the strawberries fat as teats and glossed dark as our nipples, just like Ail said. Behind us, the fountain show trickled to a piss-stream, the spouts froth-ing like rabid mouths. *Take a picture of me,* she said, and I used my phone. But the water had already bailed down into the ground, and the only thing behind her was the sky, scoured clean by skyscrapers and hotels, the cursive *B* of Bellagio crowning the night, its light thick as pus.

Ail and I, in an effort to disprove to our boss that water in the desert was made of piss, once did research about the aquifers. We printed out articles with pictures proving that each casino had its own aquifer, a sponge of holed rock through which groundwater could be extracted. Each casino corresponded to a symmetrical sea. All the water here was owned. But our boss said *the people don't want to know about aquifers* and left the kitchen to smoke. He stared for hours at the wreck of his cardboard boat, which had been systematically eaten by the raccoons. They left only a grave-sized mound of droppings. By the end of the week, he'd finished building a second boat, this time out of a kiddie pool and foam noodles, but the raccoons ate that one too, a process that repeated until it became a kind of biblical game: our boss creating the boat in six days, the raccoons consuming it in one. Our boss arrived every morning with materials scavenged from dumpsters and his own home and one time he even brought the hood of a car, which none of us were sure could float. That was how we discovered our raccoons could digest metal, because by morning the hood was translated by their mouths into a mound of metallic turds.

After the fountain show, we took a cab to New Chinatown Plaza and bought a box of strawberries from the Ranch 99. We sat cross-legged in the parking lot, waiting for raccoons to arrive, all eyes. Ail glazed the strawberries with her spit, licking its skin all over before eating it. She said this was called *sabering*. I told her she must mean *savoring*, and I wish this wasn't the last thing I remembered clearly about that night: correcting the language of her want, telling her I wanted to go home, that strawberries were my least favorite fruit, that we hadn't gone to Japan and never would.

Ail called me a pigamist. I told her she meant *pessimist*. She said no, I had the head of a pig and the soul of one, and because of that I'd never leave. I told her I didn't want to leave: there was no way to leave a place that had never been mine. Ail lapped at another strawberry and I flicked out my fingers, pinched her tongue with my thumb and forefinger, twisted it like an udder. I wanted to tear it out and bed it on rice, serve it to a stranger and never have to hear it make language. Ail invented words as if they could save her, as if each had the body of a boat, an ability to float. I thought of the boat our boss was building and how he mistook it for a body, thinking that if he began it, it would somehow grow itself, surviving like a daughter without a mother, hollowing itself to leave. They were both unbearable in their relentless self-creation, their minor godhood, Ail's hair and his boat and her mouth when I came inside it and all the sweat leapt from my skin, the salt-spray of a fountain over both our bodies.

Ail slapped me. I could tell from the funk of her sweat that she had never slapped anyone before, but that she'd been slapped herself, probably once, probably by her father when he found out the extent of her godhood: she had created her own species, renamed herself a new animal, the kind of body that loved in symmetry. Girl-girl, gone-gone, me-her. I'd always thought violence was foreign to her body, but she lifted her hand a second time and placed it on the spot she'd slapped, stroking it with her nail, and somehow I only felt the pain when she touched me like that, erasing her history from my face. Returning language to my body. She said I saw her like this city, like the fake countries along the Strip, a thing with no name of its own, a substitute want. I said I wanted to apologize.

She said *you never want to admit you want.* I said okay.

You think not wanting to leave a place is the same thing as loving it. I said okay.

You won't say that you love me, she said, batting her own voice away like a fly.

I didn't say I loved her because it was a true thing, and all my life I'd lived with falseness as a kind of skin, a shield against what was real, because what was real was adjacent to pain: what was real was blood waltzing out of your tongue when you bit it, because you were always bleeding around her, skinning a finger on a fish-gutting blade or yanking a zipper so hard and fast it caught on your pubic hair and tore it out by the root and she spent the rest of the night dabbing you with her tongue. You came from the sympathy of her spit. Vegas was a premise: nothing is native to this place, so everything can belong in it, even you. Here you could be a tourist of your own body, safe in knowing that your home was somewhere else. Somewhere you could return to, unbruised by want and with a name.

I wanted to tell Ail about my neighbor: Mrs. Tai sat every night on the balcony next to ours and ate grass jelly out of a vase. She was always eating out of things not designed to be eaten from: vases, ash trays, backpacks full of saltine sleeves. I'd once seen her eat beef noodle soup out of a bucket the size of her head. I'd once seen her drink condensed milk out of an Elmer's glue jar. She plucked a cigarette from between her breasts and lit it with a match she struck against the rusted railing. She always offered me one, but I said only my father smoked. I said I liked my teeth. Mrs. Tai's teeth were fireflies, flitting in and out of her mouth when she spoke, yellow as yolks. Every night, she liked to tell the story of how she'd almost been kidnapped: decades ago she'd been a showgirl: *the first Chinese girl to own a pair of ham-hips,* she said. She wore a nightgown with a pattern of crows on it, though later I'd see they weren't crows but an alphabet of stains. She said one night, when she was working at a geisha-themed club, a white man standing in the dark outside the dressing room had knocked her out with a crowbar. Some nights it wasn't a crowbar: it was his fist, a beer bottle, a pineapple, an electric flyswatter, a nightstick, a belt buckle, a kneecap. He taped her mouth shut and handcuffed her in the backseat, though sometimes there was no tape and she screamed, and sometimes she had hands to shatter his passenger window, to claw his face raw as steak. She said she thought he was going to dump her somewhere beside the highway, but instead he drove her all the way to the Pacific, all the way to the coast. *I was passed out*, she said, *and when I woke up, there it was: the ocean.* I asked her what happened next, but she never told me. Sometimes the man was Chinese. Sometimes the man was her father or her husband. She said she'd crawled along the beach, handcuffed, and saw two seagulls pecking something on the shore: the body of a baby seal, its skin scrolled back to expose bright fat. Ail would have asked how she made it back. Ail would have asked if she'd fought. Ail would have believed every version of the story, or at least performed a kind of math, adding and subtracting details until the sum of it was this: the sea. Mrs. Tai spat black jelly off the balcony and flicked her cigarette into the neighboring balcony's Jacuzzi. I knew she remembered nothing but the man, his hands in the dark splayed like moth wings, the way she'd smelled salt when the rod punctured the back of her head.

Another story: when I was elementary school, I was friends with a girl whose mother was a gambler. She spoke Cantonese and I understood only two things she ever said: *thank you* and *stop.* One Halloween, we both dressed up like mermaids: I drew a sea-shell bra onto a brown T-shirt and she drew nipples on hers. We wore blonde wigs from the dollar store and shell necklaces strung on twine. For a tail, we taped cellophane candy wrappers onto our legs, walking in the light where they shimmered without commitment. That night, when we were trick-or-treating in her apartment building, we'd knocked on a fifth-floor door that wouldn't answer. It was dark in the apartment, no snake of light slithering out from the door crack, so the girl and I broke in. She said she knew this apartment, knew how to hairpin the lock, how to elbow the knob at an angle and enter. Inside: no furniture, no carpet, just Jacuzzis. There was one in the bedroom, three in the living room of varying sizes, one with wood paneling glossed dark as blood, two with some kind of titanium armoring. The girl dared me to get into the biggest one, the Jacuzzi with speckled blue lining and six jets in total, the biggest body of water I'd ever been inside. The Jacuzzi was empty, but we flopped like fish at the bottom of it, impersonating mermaids, pretending to swim away from boys we'd spotted on the shore, boys who would fall in love with us and commit suicide in the sea, slitting their wrists with splinters of driftwood, dyeing the water to match the sunset. The empty Jacuzzi stank of chlorine and hardboiled eggs and we removed our tails, the cellophane wrappers crunching beneath us loud as bone. We put our wrists between each other's legs and panted and pearled with sweat and my hands were fish-raw for days, my knuckles scrubbed blank by her salt. In a few years, the girl learned English and called me a dyke, and I wanted to bring her back to that water, the water inside our bodies, and tell her yes, I was a dyke, a dam: a body built for restraint, an antonym for water. Designed to anticipate disaster, rein back rivers, bar floods. I knew what I was born for, and the girl had known it too, known where to locate the leaks in me, known where to plug her tongue and prevent me from spilling.

While I said nothing, Ail left. She got up from the blacktop of the parking lot and combed the cigarette butts from her skirt. They hung in the air like fireflies. She left me the rest of the spit-shined strawberries, and I held each one up to my nose and sniffed it, wanting to relive the last of her voice, feeling like a raccoon that had stolen something.

Ail didn't come to work the next morning. I did the work of two, slicing fish so fast and without feeling that I almost served someone a sliver of my skin. Two days later, when I finally told myself I'd search for her, a customer—white and bald as a pearl—said there'd been an Asian girl seen lingering outside the casinos without going in, and when the security guard asked her what she was doing, she asked for the way to the sea. They'd all pointed downward at the ground and I remembered the aquifers, wondering whether groundwater was saltwater or fresh, if the sea rose from the ground like sweat.

You wouldn't believe what happened, the man said. He was looking at my breasts, eyeing the left one and then the right as if trying to decide which was ripe. *Tell me,* I said, and he finally looked at my mouth, each lip individually. *She stripped,* he said. *Completely. She laid on the ground naked and the security guard had to pry her from the marble, except that her body was completely stuck. Like a magnet. They just couldn't lift her. There were like seven of them.* The man said I should tuck my hair behind my ears because my ears were dainty, like petals he wanted to put in his mouth. I walked out the restaurant without taking his order, and then I was on the Strip, realizing that I'd forgotten to ask the man which casino he'd been at, where he'd seen the girl, the Asian one, the one like me, the one who took off my shirt one shoulder before the other, kissing my bones in an order unknown to me: the heel, the ankle, the shoulder blade, the chin, the kneecap, the ball of the shoulder, the collarbone, the shin, the shin again. Back then, I shut my eyes and tried to figure out why she was doing this, why she was touching me out of order, but now I knew: she was making a place of me. She was mapping me into a city that couldn't be found.

The night I walked home from the restaurant, it rained from the ground. Water sweated up from the aquifers, up through the ground, up toward the sky. Geysers uprooted the street. The droplets, big as bullets, shot up to the highest floors of the hotels and punctured the clouds, bringing them down. In hours, Bellagio was up to its windows in water, the imitation Eiffel Tower limping on one leg after the flood-river stole away its others. I waded to the sushi restaurant and waited for Ail, trying to call her number before I remembered she didn't have a phone. I brought two umbrellas, even though I knew umbrellas were useless against rain that flew up from the ground, rain that entered through your feet and clamored up your spine. I waited for three hours, submerged to the waist in water, the slaughtered fish floating by. Outside in the parking lot, the raccoons had boarded the kiddie-pool boat our boss abandoned, and now three of them were oaring down the street with their tails. The raccoons were so wet they looked glossy, beautified by disaster, and when one the babies slipped off the prow and into the water, I saw its mother snag a claw into the rain-river and hook the baby out, a movement so practiced I wondered if the raccoons had been prepared, if Ail had warned them in advance of the rain's happening, if she had reversed gravity so that the raccoons could do exactly this: leave.

Cabs bobbed on the floodsea like metallic buoys. So many tourists drowned that the security guards of all the casinos formed a paramilitary and used their flashlights to patrol the street-river in groups of ten, scanning the floodwaters for casualties. Their flashlights could shine straight through water, hitting what used to be the street but was now the river-bottom, silted with bodies and gambling chips. My father said it was like ladling stew: the water was thick with so many bodies, so many lampposts, so many limbs and dogs and babies, that it almost made him hungry. I was the one who swam home from the restaurant and caulked every seam in our wall, every window and exit, because I knew he couldn't swim. Our apartment building—where all the dealers lived—was only safe because it detached from the ground, giving up on itself, boating on the surface of the floodwater. We woke every day in a new part of the city, under a different piece of the sky, and our daily joy was guessing where we were before we opened our eyes. Some days I thought about Ail before opening my eyes, praying she was alive, praying she was responsible for the water because otherwise it was possible she was dead, face-down or hacked to pieces by the paramilitary so that they could fit more bodies on their homemade boats, which were more architecturally advanced that any of the boats our boss had built: these boats had headlights made of flashlights, wood bodies made from glossed tables, and life-jackets made of shopping bags. When the paramilitary went by with their bags of limbs, I counted each one, as if that would somehow lower the odds that she was inside one of them, that I'd have to stitch her whole with a thread of memory, remembering which part of her body attached to the next. I thought I'd known her body like I knew my name, but I couldn't remember anything below her chin. Only her face and the way it had looked when she'd waited for me to say I loved her, or when she waited for me in the dark to kiss her, her eyes like those raccoons', oiled with hunger, bright as a salted wound.

One morning I saw the raccoons go by on their boat. I counted there were maybe sixteen, including babies. The raccoons looked skinnier, their spines written more prominently, but other than that they looked healthy. They were speaking to each other in raccoon language, which seemed to consist mostly of blinking and tail-whipping. One of the raccoons I recognized as the baby that had almost drowned, and it was squatting between its mother's legs, a bulb of milk in its mouth. Then I saw the shadow of a second boat, three times as big, bright with men: paramilitary carrying sacks of blood. The man at the prow took out a gun, some kind of pistol, and shot the raccoons one by one as they passed. The bullets were digested into their bodies, turning them into a species of holes. I could see the dark they kept in their bellies, the crumbled sugar of their bones. A few raccoons rocked into the water, shoved by the force of the bullet through their bones, but mostly they just slumped over like they were sleeping. Their tails stopped oaring and dragged through the water. I tried to see if the baby was still alive, but the bodies were indistinguishable, a shredded blanket of meat. One of the bullets pounced through my window and I ran to seal the hole in the glass before the water found it. By the time I was finished plugging the hole with caulk and glue and my own fingers, the raccoon boat was gone, and there wasn't even any blood in the river. The water had no nostalgia, no desire to witness anything but its own rise, its erasure of everything named.

I don't remember what I learned from living it and what I learned from watching the TV reports later. Months later, I watched my life from another city. They were all reruns, as if replaying the news could corral it in the past, each repetition an attempt to say it away. What I saw one morning before there were news cameras: the Ranch 99 boated up, and an auntie in pajamas stepped out of the automatic doors, right onto the surface of the river, her bag of bok choy strapped to her back like a flotation device. She swam with her hands, chin cleaving the water, paddling somewhere I don't know. A white boy went by on a water ski, but he hit the tip of a telephone pole jutting out of the water and tripped headfirst into the river, his spine limp as a necklace.

After I saw the raccoons slaughtered, I considered building a boat of my own and paddling with my hands to Ail's house. But there were no materials in the house except for my mattress and my button-down shirts and my father's collection of newspapers and the lunch meats in the refrigerator. There was a night after the reverse-rain began when my father climbed into my bed and fell asleep with his face smeared on my pillow, his body balled into a fist around my sheets. I flicked the hair from his face and stroked the back of his neck, humming a children's song I must have learned from him, about a boat that thinks the sky is an upside-down sea. Even this close, the distance between our bodies felt like the one between countries.

Ail once said you could know everything about a person by asking them for their first memory of water. She said hers was of seeing a koi fish as big as a bus. She saw it rip out of the water in Taiwan, its yellow scales each as big as the sun. The koi ate whole cows and houses and sometimes whales. One day it washed up on the beach, belly up with its whiskers long as telephone wires, and someone had to come and pierce its belly with a spear to keep it from exploding in the heat. But the koi exploded anyway, its transparent guts raining down on the town and frying brown on aluminum roofs. *It was one big barbecue,* Ail said, and for months people chiseled flesh off the koi-corpse and ate it down to its bones, which were so big they were repainted into dinosaur fossils and sent to a scam museum that displayed them.

My first memory of water wasn't a body. It was rain, but not rain like this: the rain I remembered was weak as our showerhead and intermittent, and it had been caused by my mother, who was alive in this memory and dead in all the others. She told me that the purpose of rain was to manufacture rainbows, and the purpose of a rainbow was to act as a bridge between the living and the dead. After she died, I ran outside every time it rained, which wasn't often in our drought state, and waited for my mother to walk across the rib of a rainbow and say my name. I hadn't seen any rainbows yet, but I still checked the sky daily. I still mistook the glow of oil in the floodriver for a rainbow: the breach of my mother's feet as the sky birthed her backward, returning her to me. I wanted to ask Ail what this said about me. I wanted to know if she missed me.

Next door, Mrs. Tai ate her cat. She'd spent three days knocking on every door on our floor, asking if we had any food to spare, but none of us answered. My father once said that the real difference between Americans and people like us was that Americans clustered together during disasters, and people like us played dead. My father kept cans of Spam under his bed in anticipation of sudden apocalypses, and at some point in the week we began to eat it directly out of the can, without the patty of cold rice, without using any utensils. We clawed the cold meat with our hands and nearly swallowed our fingers. Since the water shut off, we drank directly from the floodwaters, even though it gave us diarrhea for days at a time and the carpet was stained with it, a mosaic of our sickness. My father lit candles in the bedroom, but mostly we lived in the dark, waking in the day with bruises and cuts we accrued in the dark without bothering to check if we'd bled. It was today when we heard Mrs. Tai strangling her cat with the cord of her hairdryer: the cat cried like a newborn, and for a second we thought Mrs. Tai had given birth. It was a wail with the lifespan of a wind, a cry that harmonized with the rain, and when it was over the cat was dead and Mrs. Tai was planning sweet-and-sour ribs.

We heard her crying as she cooked the cat on a sheet of tinfoil, over a fire of magazines and toilet paper rolls. The cat had been her late husband's, a man who'd been an officer in the Chinese navy and who always maintained his hands in fists behind his back, as if he were holding a weapon he didn't know how to put down. His pockets sagged with sweat and strawberry candies he gave out to anyone younger than him, which was everyone. When he died, we saw Mrs. Tai's cat prancing down the hallway wearing his clothing, a sock or his watch or his old Chinese naval hat. Mrs. Tai pretended the cat had stolen them, but we knew she was dressing it. She sometimes shaved a bald spot into the back of the cat's head, symmetrical to her husband's.

We never heard from Mrs. Tai again after she ate her cat, not even when we began to evacuate, not even the night we saw the goat in the water and banged on her door, asking if she had a rope to loan us. The goat floated by our window in the morning, its white head bobbing on the water, its lips bloody and bleating. There was a sphere of flesh missing from its hind leg, a bite-wound the size of an apple. I suspected it was the sharks. No one was sure where the sharks came from, only that they fattened on eating corpses in the water. There were fish of every color that had escaped from hotel aquariums, some of them silver or striped, others marbled like meat, all of them caricaturing the sea.

My father and I hoisted the goat out by its head. We wrestled it through our window before shutting it, water already up to our ankles. The goat's udders glowed with milk, its fur paling the room. It was slimy with some kind of oil, and flies flirted with its eyes. The goat was missing an eye, perhaps eaten by a fish, and its empty socket was silver as a mirror. I slept with it in my bed that night.

Ail's house grew a pair of wasp wings, big as a Boeing's, her house flitting over my building, headed somewhere above me. I asked her where she was going. *Tokyo!* she said, and I didn't think she was kidding. She was gripping her curtains like reins, and her mother and father were both trying to close their front door, which kept mouthing open in the wind. Ail yanked on her curtains and the house flew up a few more feet, its wings razoring through clouds, its underside scabbed with soil and turf lawn. I almost thought about asking her take me too, but I didn't think her house could survive a landing, and I didn't think she needed me. I imagined her house flying over Tokyo, her head hooking out the window, her eyes turning the whole city into skyscrapers of salt, the sea soaring in to dissolve it all, the buildings, the trees, me.

Later I dreamed of flagging her down, calling her house by its name the way her grandmother called down planes, but instead I woke without language. I had to walk around my room and touch every object to learn its name again. I forgot Ail's name until it was night, the syllables worming cavities through my teeth.

My father and I moved to California to outrun the river. A month later it rained, the clouds midwifing a minor flood. But it was ordinary rain, top-to-bottom, birth-to-burial, following the same gravity as our grief. My father and I lived in a house this time, and we'd brought the goat with us. The goat was meant to eat all the weeds and dry brush and prevent wildfires from hemming us in. The day before it rained in California, the goat gave birth to a litter of dead fetuses, each of them smaller than my fist. They were stillborn because my father had been starving the mother—he thought the goat was getting fat and didn't account for procreation. The stillborn goats were nearly skinless, and I could see the wicks of their veins, blue and red and green, the rainbow bridge I was waiting to walk across. I wondered how I'd ever thought blood was just one color. My father said they were dead because the blood became stone inside them. They didn't have hearts of their own yet. Our goat bleated, licking its beard until it was salt. It had pushed out its babies so hard that its intestines were displaced, backed up into its belly. My father massaged the goat's stomach all night, coaxing the knot of its guts back into the correct cavity, and when the rain came in the morning, the goat stood up on its own in the kitchen and brayed my name so clearly I cried, the rain crystallizing to salt as it came down.

My father and I couldn't guess what had impregnated our goat until we looked closer at the fetus-skulls: attached to the sides of their heads were little black ears, flimsy as peach-skin. The neighbor's German shepherd owned black ears like that, cone-shaped ears that were so deep I couldn't imagine how sound survived the passage. *Your dog fucked our goat*, my father shouted over the fence, but only the dog answered.

I visited Vegas again when the paramilitary left and the Strip was re-flooded with filtered water, converting the desert into a water city. Ail like to remind me that all deserts were once oceans, so maybe Vegas had merely returned to its past life. The main street was an artery that spidered off into smaller canals. Every night, LED lanterns dyed the canalwater green and blue and the red of fresh blood. In the day, there were glass-bottomed boat tours and whale-watching and walkable shallows where fish nipped dead skin off the tourists' feet. I bought a baseball cap embroidered with *Venice of California* and loitered in the lobby of a Renaissance-themed hotel where all the bellhops were dressed as famous European artists. A man dressed as Michelangelo was fondling a Chinese woman's furred suitcase like he was sculpting it. I thought about the time Ail and I snuck onto the rooftop pool of the Oriental, rubbing the jade Buddha in the lobby for good luck and riding the elevator to the one-hundredth floor, pretending to be Chinese heiresses misbehaving without our husbands.

On the roof, the pool was bright as a coin lying on its side. There were six white women lying in bleached lawn chairs, slack as slaughtered fish, oiled brown from their ankles to their wrists. Ail looked at me with the sky unpinned behind her, veiling her face like lace. The crows were mating on the rooftop, and two men carrying pond fronds beat the birds back before they could shit in the pool or dapple the deck. Ail stepped forward, slicking back her

Spring 2021 ♀ 227

hair with spit: *ready?* I wanted to ask *for what?* But Ail had already fired me backward into the pool, both hands shoving against my chest, my ribs flexing like bowstrings. I landed inside a pupil of water, the round bottom of the pool waxing into a moon. I saw her from below the surface, her body upside down above me, her teeth where her eyes should be, her ears winging her head and flying away. Her face was borderless, wavering behind panes of water, and already she was farther from me than my mother. By the time I surfaced, Ail was in the water with me, hula-hooping her hips, warming the water with her piss. Then security came and hauled us out, our bodies wetter than when we were born, and escorted us into the elevator wearing borrowed robes.

I tried counting how many years ago her face was. I wore my new baseball cap low over my brow. When I crossed the lobby, counting the bruised floor tiles arranged in the shape of the Vesuvius Man, I saw Ail enter through the glass doors ahead. The glass doors were so thick they acted as a magnifying glass, streaming the sun outside into the size of the sky itself. Two motorboats bobbed against the street curb, both of them painted the color of flayed salmon. She was wearing a skirt made of some flammable material, silver and holographic and so thin I could see each individual wrinkle in her knees. Her sunglasses were studded with crystals I knew were real from the way light lingered inside them instead of passing straight through. She was with a woman, a woman who looked like us but who'd never gone by any name but her own. Ail tugged on a leash so thin it looked like a strand of spit. It was attached to the collar of a mottled Chihuahua, its legs thin as my fingers. I almost waved, but she had already passed me, and the woman at her side leaned in, licking Ail's neck with a thirst I'd seen in no other species.

When I reached the glass doors, I turned around and Ail was thumbing the elevator button. Sweat throttled my hair in its hands. She got on. I said her name across the lobby. Her face found mine like a thrown knife. Outside, water rose up from the canals in a whip, lashed the buildings skinless, the sky slender as the slit in a fishbelly. It was raining again, raining rock-salt that knocked out of the teeth of tourists and tenderized the windows into nightmeat. Ail and I walked toward each other, my hand in a fist, a salute to the dark inside her. Her mouth beached against mine and our spit knit together, enough fabric for a flood. Outside, the water fist-pumped toward the sky, reaching our knees, our necks. Light spearing us through the lungs. When the water came up over our heads, we breathed the air we'd stored in each other and stayed under.

2

Crystal Ke

FEI

Crystal Ke

LIFE

Crystal Ke

NVSHEN

Crystal Ke

IN CONVERSATION WITH VI KHI NAO

Crystal Ke

VI KHI NAO: One could see the limitation(s) in working with a limited medium, black and white. Your work is profoundly intricate and provocative and (if I may add, narrative). I am curious as to how you are able to develop your form. And, has visual art been your primary vehicle of expression or have you dabbled in other disciplines as well? And, what is your relationship to those other mediums?

CRYSTAL KE: I have actually never taken an art class before, except for Chinese calligraphy as a child. Even back then, the smell of the ink and the meditative motion of mixing it in the stone entranced me. Black and white has been my favourite means of creation ever since. I was tempted to study art in university, but always managed to talk myself out of it. Instead, I studied economics, non-profit management, and international development. Ironically, I think it was the best decision I could have made for my development as an artist. I was forced to confront so many problems with the world that I could not address through policy or bureaucracy. But I could in art. In art I found my voice.

VKN: What are some of those problems, Crystal?

CK: The limitations society puts on the female form, be it forms of expression or choice.

VKN: How long did it take you to create "NVSHEN"? Is that the title of your piece? I love the sorrowful details you asserted on the repetitive faces of the female form. There is also so much textural depth to your background. You introduced gray to it and it propels it forward into a floating, riparian three-dimensionality. Was the artistic gesture intuitive or did you play around with some monochromatic colors before settling on the grayness? Can you talk about how the drawing arrived to you? Where were you in life when you gave birth to it?

CK: "NVSHEN" is the pinyin spelling of 女神, meaning goddess. At the time, I was creating a zine called *Heartstrings* based off a dream I had about the loneliness of being multicultural and without roots. Meanwhile, I was going through a heartbreak that only reinforced this feeling that I did not belong in one category or another. The grey represents that space in between, where so many under-represented people live their lives. The gesture was intuitive, and I did not try out other colours or shades of grey.

VKN: Repetition, fluidity, and sensuality seem to be the central driving force of your submitted pieces. May I ask if sapphicity or sapphic sexuality have a major role in influencing the language of your creativity? Or are these three primary forces emerge as a result of your relationship/intimacy with femininity/masculinity?

CK: I was raised in a very masculine household and did not see myself as female when I was younger. However, I was always very intrigued and titillated by the female form. Growing up in Hong Kong, I was surrounded by images of nude women. Magazines were available in every 7-Eleven, and porn theatres had big advertisements. These images did not portray the softness or strength of women that I love. I like the symbol of circles—cycles, the moon, infinity, etc. But I also love the hypnotic effect of mandalas. I feel like I'm trying to brainwash the viewer into loving soft bodies.

VKN: Regardless of my sexual orientation, I will admit that I willingly and thoroughly allow my brain to be washed by your creativity. If the viewer is seduced into loving soft bodies, what do you think the viewer should do with that love?

CK: I think it comes down to normalizing, rather than fetishizing, different bodies. This means allowing them to exist as something beautiful, something to be respected, rather than just barely tolerated. This also goes into a more macro view of wanting to change the perception of society, which can hopefully lead to changes in policy and changes in culture. Especially coming from an East Asian background, it is difficult to validate your existence as a fat woman without constantly having to apologize to complete strangers.

VKN: I was very drawn to how inclusive and organic you limn the female form. How voluptuous and natural you depict them. De-anorexicizing the female form in your work is one way of transforming the way viewers gaze at women; what other female expressions (that society frowns upon, rejects) do you wish to embrace in your work? What other projects do you have in mind for your future artistic efforts? Would you ever pursue the medium of film?

CK: I appreciate the full spectrum of the female form. I do not limit myself to drawing only one body type, and often depict various vaginal secretions (such as menstrual blood, etc.). I have not worked with film; however, my previous exhibitions have been mixed media rather than illustration. For my exhibition *Still Bound*, I made small lotus shoes from modern trendy materials—lace, leather, etc. They were photographed with other items that still bind Chinese women today. I am starting a residency at the Dali Art Factory in November. My goal is to expand my artistic vocabulary to include more traditional art mediums that will allow me to better articulate inequality where I see it.

VKN: Have you done nude men?

CK: I have done nude trans-men and trans-women, but not nude cis-men.

VKN: Would you have liked to marry your different professional impulses into one? Where you are able to economize sensuality? Non-profit manage femininity? Internationally develop soft bodies? What would that global landscape of beauty look like?

CK: No. Those industries are toxic and pollute art. However, I do believe that respect for all women, regardless of sexual orientation, body type, and ethnicity, is something that desperately needs to be implemented in all industries.

VKN: Can you talk about your piece "Fei"? Like all or most of your submitted work, it's very startlingly playful and pelagic. Almost a departure from your other pieces—though I could still see remnants of your quintessential traits of waves, clouds, circles, and vectors of sultriness and carnality in it. What do you hope for viewers to walk away with from "Fei"? I am particularly drawn to the kidney-shaped lips of the fish, bearing emotive expressions of startledness and awe. And, the fish's fins bear resemblance to wings of birds. As if you gave them wings in order to unchain, de-incarcerate them from water, give them a new, survivable relationship to air. What was your emotional impulse behind this piece?

CK: I drew this piece while at the Red Sea. The sun was setting in a way where there was no separation between sea and sky. I have always loved the blending of land and sea—probably due to my childhood on Hong Kong island. But that was the first time I saw them merge like that. I was awestruck and immediately set about trying to capture it. Fei, 飞, is "Fly" in Mandarin. The ocean has always been a source of freedom for me, but this piece represents the illusion of boundaries and borders.

VKN: Speaking of fish and sea which make me think of food. What did you have for lunch today, Crystal? What is your favorite dish? Do you love to cook?

CK: I was working on a mural today and didn't have time to eat. Food is my second great love. My favourite food is probably durian. I also love anything from every part of Asia and the Mediterranean. Cooking is one of my biggest passions—lately I've been in the forests of Western Massachusetts, where I've been foraging different fungi. I've been experimenting with chaga, black trumpets, and chanterelle mushrooms.

VKN: Oh, no. Would you like to take a break and eat? Or snack on something? I am around to interview you and I am in no great rush. I devote today just to interview you. I love durian too. And, I don't quite get why it's banned from public venues like Ubers and airports and hotels. The smell is what shapes the experience of me loving this particularly decadent fruit. It's like asking a woman to have sex without an orgasm. It's unforgivable.

CK: Don't worry! I've been snacking on an apple scone that a friend brought for me. Re: durian. Oh, I know! Durian is delicious, and smells amazing to me. I'm hoping to spend a May or June at a durian farm in Malaysia soon. Being able to just make art, cook, swim, and taste different strains of durian just sounds like a dream to me.

VKN: Can you talk about your first carnal and emotional experience with being with a woman? What was it like? Were you assertive? How old were you? What is your courtship with women like? I don't know how to court women. I always feel that machines (dishwashers, blenders, coffee makers) tend to break down when I court a woman. I have learned to be passive. Mechanical things tend to operate better when I am not so assertive.

CK: I am bisexual, but I'm not very physically attracted to men. Some of my earliest memories from toddlerhood were hiding away secret photos of naked women so that my family wouldn't see my collection. The first time I was physically with a woman was when I was fifteen. It was the first time I enjoyed a kiss. I am a loud and assertive person in most areas of my life, but terribly shy in courtship. I don't know how to court men or women. They just usually approach me and have to be incredibly direct before I get the message. However, as soon as it's clear that there is an attraction, I'm back to my assertive self. I also attended a Mormon university (Brigham Young University) where "homosexual activity"—or any pre-marital activity—is grounds for expulsion. I was there from ages sixteen to twenty, which are very formative sexual years for a person. Because of this, I always hid my sexuality . . . which is probably why I find courtship so difficult.

VKN: Ah, I understand. You know, I am told that one's formative sexual years also get reincarnated in a female's late thirties and early forties. If such a reincarnation were to take place in your body, what would you like to do with it? And, what do you mean by not being very physically attracted to men? And, how do you define bisexuality?

CK: My personal definition of bisexuality is actually pansexuality. I am emotionally attracted to certain personality traits regardless of gender. However, unless I'm emotionally attached to a man, I generally won't find them physically sexually attractive. I am an extremely sexual person. I just am not very public about it because of my years at BYU. Because of that, I'm also notoriously bad at realizing when someone is flirting with me. I hope I'll be continuing to have a lot of amazing sex until the day I die!

VKN: I hope you continue to, too! Maybe even in the chthonian world as well! In art, your preferred color choices are black and white and potentially gray. In life, what colors are you most drawn to?

CK: For myself? Always black, white, and grey. That's true for my art, my clothing, my physical environment . . . But that changes very quickly when it comes to others. For example, I'm very attracted to bright, vivid colours: teals, corals, jewel tones, etc. when it comes to someone else's art or clothing.

VKN: The women in your drawings are all individualistic in their ontological composition. They repeat and multiply, but their bodies are not coupled or intertwined erotically/romantically. Have you created pieces in which there are two women who are fastened or intimate with one another not as a group, but as a couple?

CK: In my submitted piece, Life from the Red Sea, the women are linking arms. My art features nudity, but I'm not trying to be sexual. I'm just trying to normalize the natural act of being nude, vulnerable, and free.

VKN: Am I correct to observe that you desire universal expression of female sexuality, as a cosmic entity?

CK: Almost. I desire universal expression of the female form as a cosmic entity—not necessarily attached to sexuality. I think the nude woman is too often associated with sex, so I try to stay away from that.

VKN: Ah, I see.

CK: I like the women in my art to be viewed as honest, open, free of judgement and societal pressure/norms. I happen to also perceive their bodies as sexy, but that's not my purpose.

VKN: Yes, I have a better contextual sense of your artistic vision and mission. Are there other artists whose work you love? Who are those folks? And, why do you love what they do?

CK: There are too many to list! Lately I've been obsessed with Victo Ngai (Instagram: @victongai). The content and colour palettes of her illustrations are just mesmerizing. I also love Toshio Saeki. His illustrations are very obviously coming from a male gaze that is objectifying, and violent towards, women. Yet something about them makes me very drawn to them. Maybe that's something I need to unpack . . .

VKN: I just checked out Ngai's work and it's super gorgeous and polychromatic and verdant! Saeki's work is violent indeed. But perhaps you were drawn to his work because he doesn't censure the unreflective urges of his imagination. He just displays them nonchalantly, almost casually on the page without shame or apology. On a more practical note, what advice would you give other Asian women about their bodies, their art, and especially their relationship to time?

CK: Question everything you believe about yourself, and stop giving a fuck. I found that digging deep into the history of policy, borders, and culture really helped me realize how unimportant and fleeting current ideals are. There's no reason to be bound by them.

STRENGTH IN SOFTNESS
Whitney Romberg-Sasaki

Photo Credit: Whitney Romberg-Sasaki

Artist Statement

My art practice is informed by ideas of queer, feminine resilience. I seek to challenge society's ideas of what it means to be strong. With a focus on queer femme women of color, my work represents the stories and lives of women at the intersection of these demographics. In so doing, I aim to raise up queer, femme women of color in a world where we are often excluded. In this way, the women depicted in my drawings look like me. These drawings aim to celebrate these women in their own image, free from the male gaze that has long held them back. My art makes use of intersectional subjects, symbolism, and fantasy to communicate body positivity, self-love, and strength from the point of view of women who are often denigrated for displaying the same. My work has been strongly influenced by the first-person, intimate, and downright subversive themes of some of my favorite creators. In particular, I am inspired by the street art of Margaret Kilgallen, Alma López, and Johanna Toruño, as well as the graphic novels of MariNaomi. These artists have incredibly diverse experiences as women. In addition, they are artists who regularly depict the female form through the lens of their own personal experiences, relationships, and the objects that they hold dear. My body of work is similarly autobiographical. The figures in my work are contemplative, and the thought bubbles that accompany them give viewers a window into their inner desires, self-image, and body image. They are imperfect in proportion, shown with body hair and stretch marks. Rather than be restrained by these things, the characters look within, liberating themselves from a society that objectifies them. My body of work also aims to reclaim symbols and imagery often associated with fragility, transforming these into symbols of strength and resilience in femininity. One way I achieve this is through my characters' backdrops. The landscapes that they find themselves in help ground them, giving them the endurance to stay strong. Flowers and succulents in my pieces represent this resilience symbolically: these plants constantly regenerate, even if they have been nearly destroyed. Just as flowers and succulents tirelessly reinvent themselves to survive, my characters are able to remain centered in a world that tries to throw them off-balance. My inspiration for this body of work stems from my own experience as a queer woman of color who has not seen many people like me in art and media. There is a need for representation of the unique, seldom-told stories of queer, multiracial women. This is the main reason why I wish to pursue graduate studies as I research these various themes. Professionally, I hope to use my work to continue lifting up the voices of these communities as we continue to fight for representation in the current political climate. Part of the fantasy of my works is that they represent a space where queer femmes of color are safe and are celebrated for being true to themselves. My work has necessarily challenged popular ideas of what "feminine," "queer," and "strong" look like. In the end, I seek to reclaim narratives of femininity, strength and queerness, to the end that people like me will be represented.

Photo Credit: Whitney Romberg-Sasaki

A REBELLION IN REVERSE

Ross Tugade

I

"So, anong meron sa Iligan?" ("So what's there to do in Iligan?"), a friend from university once asked me.

"Ilagan," I corrected him. "Iligan is in Mindanao; my hometown Ilagan is located way up northern Philippines." Once I have made necessary rectification, his mind has already shifted to the next topic of the latest episode of a science fiction TV show.

I don't blame him. As a sore thumb of a provincial kid that stuck out in an elite university for four years, the clarification was always necessary. I learned to adapt through a dispassionate turn of phrase: I was born and raised in Isabela province, and yes, that's near Tuguegarao. The omission of Ilagan altogether, which I considered internally as a sin, was essential—I would have already provided a clearer map in the mind of whoever I was talking to once I wedged the place in between more familiar names.

Who knows how many parcels bound for Ilagan have made their way to Mindanao? I know at least of one item my sister bought online that accidentally ended up in Iligan instead of our doorstep. The frequent interchangeability of names could very well just be a random accident of nomenclature. Yet we Ilagueños take pride in the origins of our little city: we sprung from the revolt of hot-blooded men and women who refused to pay tribute to their then-new colonial masters.

The Gaddang Revolt, as it was to be known later on, caused a resettlement among our forebears. Their new community was to be named as a reminder of their transgression: Ilagan, backwards for "nagali" or the Ybanag word for "moved" or "transferred."

To answer my friend's question, the internet lists a grand total of five places to see in Ilagan: the Fuyot Springs National Park, a natural sanctuary; the Abuan River; the giant *butaka* (a hardwood-made native armchair); the Japanese wartime tunnels, where visitors can opt to wear kimonos (in dubious fashion) while making their way through the caverns; and the Queen Isabela Park.

There is only one open and commanding national highway that traverses the texture of the town—from vast corn fields to all the essential shops one needs to be familiar with as a resident. There was the Good Luck dry goods store owned by a Chinese couple, Mang Pepe's Xerox center, and the bank my mother worked in where I spent many happy days after school.

Ever since Ilagan became a city in 2012, a McDonald's burger is now always within reach. But for sixteen years of my life before moving to Manila, San Antonio's Burger Hauz burgers would be a local high schooler's definition of happiness: a piece of patty slathered with ketchup and mayonnaise, with a chunk of processed cheese and two cucumber slices all sandwiched in between a bun of dinner rolls. Pair it with their twenty-peso mango fruit shakes and the next school day's project deadlines would momentarily be suspended in memory.

II

Memory can be a curious object especially with the varying speed of the passage of time. I remember Ilagan as if I lived there long before I was born, in the cursed house of my great grand-parents with all its thirteen foundations that brought nothing but grief to some of my kin. I recall *Lolo* Adol and *Lola* Acion in the hand-me-down stories of their large brood that included the mother of my own mother. We would come to live in that same house and set up shop in a bakery where I, as a baby, would sit on display along with the breads. We would come to avoid the curse when my Manileño of a father decided to move us to another part of town.

Being half an outsider has sometimes made me question the fire of sentimentality burning through my chest. I cannot speak Ilokano nor Ybanag, though I can understand bursts of conversation. To accommodate my father and his—along with my mother's—desire to raise cosmopolitan children, we spoke Tagalog exclusively at home. I could very well have been raised in my father's Project 6 and would probably have the same tongue as I have now.

Yet growing up in Ilagan has wired me differently in ways I could never have been had I been raised elsewhere. Of course, the same probably goes for every place, but I can only speak for myself and my own understanding of the world. I ate all my vegetables and all the Ilokano dishes my mother would serve—a feat my father would only be able to accomplish later on in his life. Gastronomically, I am the child of my mother, content with feasting on raw tomatoes sprinkled with either salt or *bagoong* (fish sauce).

In the first house my father had built for us, there was a sprawling line of Indian trees in the garden. Its seeming vastness was enough for me to imagine a forest. The driveway was wide enough for me to channel the open road while I rode my bike. We eventually moved to the suburbs in my second year of high school, but I will always recall the days spent in that small bungalow. We had an imposing gate that kept other children away, which made me keep to myself in the process. A travelling salesman went to our house once and later that afternoon; hardbound books with blue and red spines were laid out for me to set my hungry eyes on. In the small corner of our living room was the universe—its secrets revealed in pages, seen through the wandering mind of a five-year-old.

Knowledge presses on, and so do the legs of a child that stretch out with time.

I recently visited the house of my childhood and found the same driveway too narrow now to fit two cars side-by-side. The Indian trees were now gone and the length where they used to sprawl out, to my own disbelief, was only a few meters in reality. For a time, that house was enough to be the world. As my father kept us away from the perils of childhood, so too, I was kept from an early understanding of how unforgiving the world can be. Books can teach the scale of hardness of minerals, or the types of energy that exist in the universe. Yet books could not save me from my first bout of loneliness away from home, from my first great heart-break courtesy of a girl with sleepy eyes.

When we moved houses, things felt a lot more complicated despite the sheen of new money and simplicity of suburban life. We actually had friendly neighbors. The large gate was gone. Each household had a cute dog. But what I took from the old house were habits that already hardened like rock: my isolation, my love for books and music, and my aloofness to people (especially to my mother's friends). Discovering that I liked girls, too, I spent much of those years hiding behind stringing a guitar and stringing words together.

I spent afternoons cataloging my parents' cassette collection, with a partiality to the boxed Beatles set and *The Best of Queen*. I would get my fill of new music from CDs bought during our monthly trips to Manila. In the airwaves of Ilagan, I would blast away what's musically in vogue in the big city. The disruption felt like a rebellion—in a few years I would be moving away from the humdrum provincial life and into the arms of a metropolis where I *knew* I belonged. A town that dimmed its lights after nine in the evening was no place for me to live. The lights of Manila waited for me, where life never went on hold.

III

My forebears carried with their legacies the shadow of a re-volt. Movement was their punishment. My ennui in the city con-firms my descent from the bloodline of rebels: my movement was also my cross to bear. The loss of my childhood and the de-sire to trade my soul to have another go at it keeps me up at nights. What can we truly fish out of our minds but fragments? It is a law of nature: time only ever moves forward.

Our hometowns can transform into anything as a function of our memories; in my case, it is a glass house full of the romance of childhood. A thing of beauty on the outside, but too fragile to even attempt to return to.

I used to have a lover who agreed that everything about me reverts to the early days of my life. Maybe she is right. My convenient references to my childhood and my hometown cover up the woundedness that life gave me. To be battered so badly by the world merits a return to innocence, to the arms of where we first learned love.

In Ilagan, it is convenient and possible to classify people according to which school they went to, the village they resided in, and even to which extended families they belonged. In the city, I am no one but myself, a mass of flesh and memory that can unravel anytime.

When things get bad, they go and turn for the worse. Yet even when the worst hits home, the familiar gives a protective barrier. Ilagan has learned to set its lights open even after nine o' clock. I, too, have learned that the dark of the early years of our lives illumines the present like no other. Sometimes, no truer words can be said but "It's good to be home."

TIMELINES

Miki Schumacher

C ivil Dusk— *7:45 p.m.*

If I turn my head to the horizon, I can just make out the shine of Venus emerging from the setting sun's pink. What is it about the night sky that always makes us feel small?

"Did you know that there are three stages of twilight? Astronomical, civil, and nautical— the middle, that's my favorite." We're holding hands and walking down a San Jose boulevard. It's been miles and my eyes grow heavy with seasonal allergies, but you promised to show me all your best bubble tea. Everything is so far apart here—distant. You lead me through the storefront, and once again I am confronted with endless choices of milk tea. I was never good at reading menus. "What do you want?"

A shy half-smile peeks out from my indecision. "Mung bean." I've had this every day I've been here. "I can't get this flavor in Minneapolis, and I'm only here for one more week." This is true. I don't say it, but another reason is that the taste reminds me of my mother's ginisáng monggó. She hasn't cooked for me since I brought another woman home. This, too, can be described as distance.

My memories find themselves poking out through food associations. Ginisáng monggó reminds me of cold winter mornings in rural Minnesota. Lumpia makes me think of late nights peeling spring roll wrappers apart for my mother. Taiwanese bread and bubble tea now make me think of you.

I find myself today trying to cook food where I don't fit. In my apartment kitchen, my kaldereta or sinigang or cassava cakes never come out like my mother's. Maybe the walls have yet to be saturated with the smell of fish sauce, or maybe my memories of home betray me. It is too much of a cruel balancing act; my brownness incompatible in queer spaces, my queerness incompatible in brown spaces. But this, this is new. I envision my identity as two old friends having come together for dinner for the first time in years. There is lots of catching up to do.

We sit outside and watch as the pink sky meets blue. The evening is cool and the air is still. Is this something I could call home?

Hesitation sits deep in my throat. I was taught denial from a young age; that to want is selfish, and therefore must be pushed down. I want to tell you everything here, but it chokes out of necessity. There is still so much I have left to say.

"I have to go back."

Nautical Dusk— 8:10 p.m.

Kissing you makes my lips buzz and my cheeks flush. Do you feel the same? Do you feel the rush, the slowness, the anxiety, the comfort all at once? I suppose airport security isn't the best place for me to pose these questions.

"Two years. Let me know where you're at then, and if this is something you want to try."

"This being . . . Us?"

You nod. "Us."

Is it idealistic of me to think that things can stay the same; that I can come back to you and still feel belonging? Is my writing then just a desperate cry for permanence, if only for a moment? This is to suspend us in amber, to pickle us in vinegar. I wonder if time will turn us golden or sour. Sappho, didn't anyone tell you how dangerous it is to live with your heart so full of longing? Please, let our companionship be more than a matter of place and timing.

Astronomical Dusk— *10:39p.m.*

Tell me, is it at dusk or dawn that we begin dreaming...

Hidden, tell me again about the twilight
Tell me the stages of beginnings and endings
of all the stars in between.
I will tell you of winter and snowfall
slow stillness of waiting in transition.
The sun sets once more below memory's shores
I will meet you again
I promise.

QUEERING TEMPORALITY

Yuri Sakakibara

My name is Yuri Sakakibara, and I am a graphic designer, artist, and recent graduate from UCLA's Design | Media Arts BFA program. I am a Japanese-American woman who has spent her years growing up in Japan, Hawaii, and then Los Angeles. My recognizing of my personal Japanese and queer identity while residing in Los Angeles has significantly influenced my aesthetic and stylistic choices, as well as what contextual subjects drive my personal work. I also have an interest in utilizing my practice within and beyond the scopes of visual art for mutual aid and community-centered organizing.

Queering Temporality is a video triptych on the topic of queerness in the context of my perceived Past, Present, and Future. The physical form of the triptych alludes to Christian three-panel paintings, juxtaposing and directly confronting the historical blaspheming of LGBTQ+ presence, as well as the remaining tension and violence against the community today. The installation is made up of three vertically placed monitors that simultaneously play found and self-recorded footage with reference to LGBTQ+ history, personal memories, and speculative world-building. The three screens are synchronized in a constant loop, paralleling one another in theme or topic, with audio clips of the scenes overlapping to form a convoluted and fused tone. Occasionally scenes of the Past seep into the Future and vice versa, demonstrating the "queering" of a linear understanding of space and time. In one scene of this video piece, I reference the traditional Japanese theater art form, Kabuki, by paralleling a clip of a man applying full makeup with myself directly mimicking his practice. Interested in the dichotomy between a traditional art form and its prominent gender-bending performance, I wanted to create a third and speculative depiction of how Kabuki can exist with queer futurism. I wanted to offer present and future Japanese Americans (and Japanese people everywhere) a vision of how we can take traditional practices and reshape them into an adapted form of gender expression that values the tradition, yet values liberation to gender expression.

Full video and description of the piece can be found at: https://vimeo.com/343862742

Made with the love and care of Grace Kim Howard, Akari Takahashi, Gelare Khoshgozaran, Sarah Rara, Jack Turpin, and Sam Congdon.

QUEERING TEMPORALITY

Yuri Sakakibara

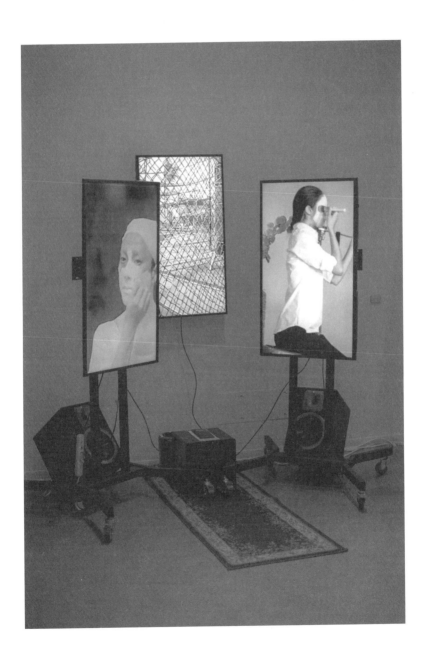

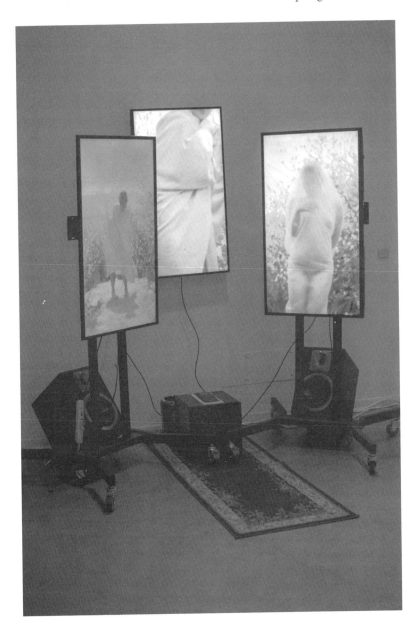

WHERE DO THE SHADOWS GO?

Yuri Sakakibara

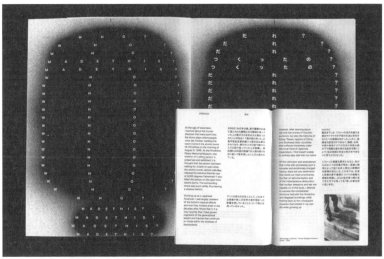

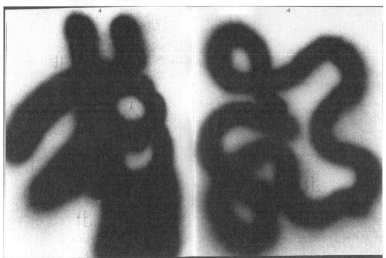

"Where Do the Shadows Go?" is a two-part informational book and personal narrative on the Hiroshima and Nagasaki atomic bombings in August of 1945.

This book considers these events not only from the perspective of atomic bomb victims, but also evaluates 20th century Imperial Japan from the perspectives of the countries it occupied, seeking to present a nuanced portrait of a complex and painful period of time. Interspersed throughout the historical sections, I also present a third perspective: that of my own, as a Japanese American woman attempting to navigate and reconcile a history that is at once distant and all too close to home, and one that seems to yield no clear-cut answers for someone caught in between.

The passages are each sectioned into numbered topics in the booklet and have corresponding spray paint paintings as abstract expressions of each sentiment in the larger picture book. The essays were originally written in English and translated into Japanese by myself, then reviewed and edited by Grace Kim Howard.

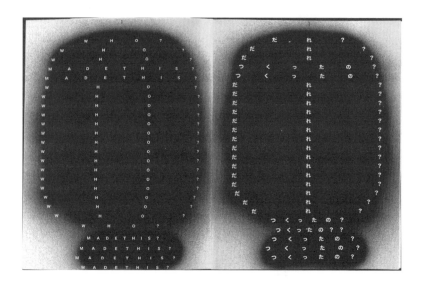

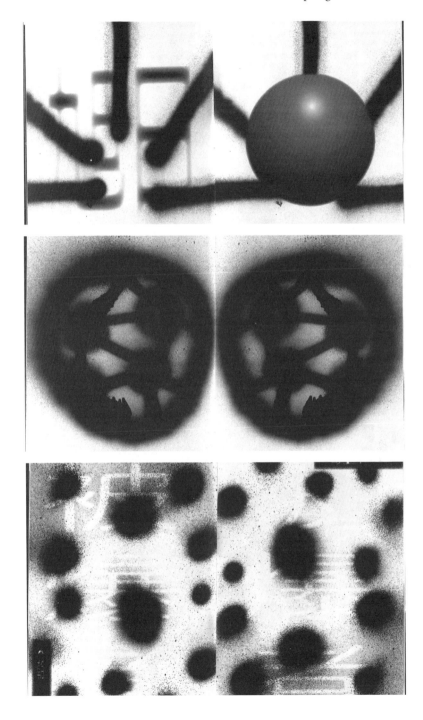

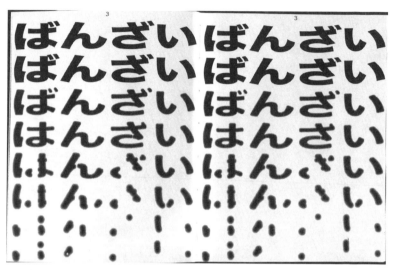

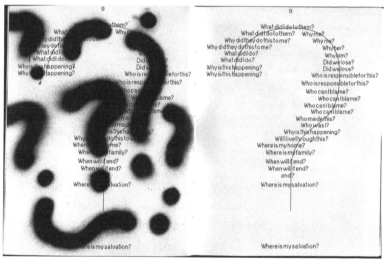

NOTES FROM A CLOSET

Orchid Wen

When your body is a closet, it can feel safer to stay closed. You move through the world seen as a passive vessel, there to store the belongings of others. No one knows what you have in there. They think takeout menus, Chinatown fans, nail polish, and massage oil. They don't guess mirror, shield, magic wand. They don't guess radio, safety net, and communist femmifesto. You're just forgotten square footage, not worth calling a room. Barely there.

Your friend Tiff once brought you to a store in the Haight Ashbury, full of taxidermied things with bones that once felt flesh. It felt uncanny to you, not because the frozen weasel or beetle were so familiar, but because it felt like what you thought your closet might look like if borne to a public. A family of moths, fed on felted blue wools, and light like fine hair electrified by static. The sticky slab of brown who-knows-what from who knows how long ago, next to a pair of chopsticks, with it a smell of dinge. A thick orange blanket, built for cold weather on the mainland but now contorted in its insulation of the California dark. A Vornado fan, with dust like yarn. An ancestor of the modern computer. A dissertation, multiple. Somewhere, photographs. Elsewhere, your diaries. These items create your internal gallery, you the curator. Then there are the stacks of unlabeled files, abandoned for a future rest day, an occasional postcard thrown in here or there, evidencing sun baked buttes and magnificent metallic structures, faded sentiments of care and being missed, of gel pens and once iridescent inks, puffy stickers of anthropomorphized avocados and fuzzy ones of cartoon Pomeranians. The world reveals itself in these details protected by your closet, and you observe, you take note, and you archive.

The list would be long, ongoing, a closeted hoarder, a horde full of closets. It's a marvel you can go anywhere, brittle in your foundation as you stand, weighted by your generations of heavy goods. And yet you do, you carry yourself with you. You carry your closet with you for you are yourself and your self is a closet.

Some closets are cabinets. As a child you delighted in playing hide and seek along the upstairs corridor of your maternal grandparents' home in the South Bay. In one, some stacked bedsheets; in another, plastic-covered photo albums banished from the light. You'd open and let go in order to hear the soft return of the rectangular door on its matching frame, a restful posture, the dark wood so calming. The last door in the row had a trap in it that you liked to taunt; the last cabinet was a laundry chute, with a cut-out square just small enough that your kid frame could not fit all the way through. When you were brave, you dangled a leg down, your weight bent over the other leg, and it was because of the cool quiet that you could summon the courage, learning to trust sensation rather than vision in the threat of engulfment.

Your elementary school classmate Katherine lived in a mansion in the hills, as big as any of the ones you had seen in the wealthy suburb your parents bought a shack in before your father died. During a sleepover, Katherine walked to the sliding doors of her closet at bedtime. She revealed its packed contents and said, "See, there's nothing inside." You understood that she meant, no monsters. You slept with some relief, because when you lay in bed or the folded duvet you called a sleeping bag and no longer had your glasses on, the world took shapes that leered at you and velcroed you into a world of shadows.

You remember simple secrets as a cabinet. The cupboard under the living room sink was a toy closet, what would later be condensed to a shoebox of your Happy Meal toys, the favorite being the Looney Tunes double-sided cars with the characters you can no longer name. The stoop was the perfect height for you, tiny, the bottom step meeting your waistline when you sat, so the wee cupboard could house your menagerie of plastic goodies and glass marbles, and the perpendicular flooring the stage on which you would caravan your toys or waddle the Barbies to face one another as friends, or something more.

Sometimes you want to say, do not store your things in me. Do not enter. Beware: Dog. Hazardous Waste. Enter at your own risk. Closed. Closed shop. Closed for renovation. Closed for good. Caution: I'm at work. Caution: deer crossing. Bicycles. Child at play. No trespassing.

When you graduate from the Bay Area and move to New York City, you learn that seasons mean wardrobe diversity, meaning you need somewhere to store your coats and scarves in the summer, and somewhere to hide away your shorts and tanks in the long winter, when such clothes would seem ridiculous, as of an alien wardrobe. Opening a closet was like being shown your other body.

You've heard of people renting closets in Manhattan, just needing an address and a place to sleep. You, on the other hand, had a moldy basement room in Brooklyn with an empty closet, staring at you like an open mouth. What could you bring from across the country but bedding? August did not require things to be hung and you had no things to store except luggage, now emptied. You bought plastic coat hangers from Target as an aspirational gesture, but you grew up in a house of folded cotton, no iron or hangers required. Was it the negative space that made you think it could feel like home?

When you bring your closet with you, and you speak as a closet, like Superman is Clark Kent is the telephone booth, you could live on the other side of the country and be talking to your mom, wishing to tell her something, something significant. You've fallen in love and your world has changed. But how do you listen to a closet? And how do you talk when you are a closet? You didn't know it could be okay. Closets are not taught people skills, how to share the cobwebs when you've found them so stunning that you wouldn't dare dust, each fly carcass something to protect.

The room you share with the love of your life has two closets. On top of hers during the day lies the blackout curtain that drapes over your window at night. She sleeps best in darkness, while your mom raised you with a bright lamp directly over your dreaming head. Sometimes you fall back into bed after walking the dog, while she's at work repairing bikes, and you play a game in your head where there is something on the other side and you're not sure what. You note how nice it feels to not picture the big-eyed villain who has been with you now for decades, who appears when you shower or who hovers and listens while you practice piano. Her closet protects you somehow from this nemesis who you fear will stare you to death. Sometimes you walk past and your wind kicks up a corner enough to see her suitcase, a silent threat. After she's moved out (don't worry, her books remain), you note how your closet stores the bed linens and hers the luggage (now moved, too).

In the new empty-nest house, your mom knocked down one of two hallway closets to make space for a master bathroom on the other side. No one misses the storage space because that waterfall showerhead feels *nice*. Plus, the renovation motivated some clothes purging. Your mom still has two or three closets of colorful and patterned clothes with names of the various stores you grew up accompanying her to: Talbots, Ann Taylor, Eileen Fisher, Chico's. You hope that hidden deep in the closet, wrapped in tan plastic garment casing, remains the orange polyester fireworks dress she wore to her wedding banquet with your father in 1979. She let you borrow it once when you were a summer intern at the regional theater, for the opening night gala of *Harold & Maude: The Musical*. You loved the feeling of retro glamour, dressing up in a history you'd never known, a moving line she'd been ripped out of by grief.

You go to a closet convention where there's a sign that says group therapy outside. You don't know whether this is the best thing you've ever done or the thing that will end you. Maybe you know that the thing you want most in the world will light all that you have been on fire, and you grew up in drought country.

In the room you shared with your mother growing up, the closet was hers, with bags full of things along the floor the only things you had the height to access. You liked the feeling of curtains of fabric on your skin, weighing on your scalp, reminding you of weekends shopping with your mother and finding yourself in the middle of a circular clothes rack, sitting there with extra buttons in your palm. You don't know how you got there. Someone's hands would part the curtain of tagged blouses and soon you wouldn't know if you were in trouble. Finding these buttons was your own game. Your mother's bedroom closet was also something else, since its darkness would threaten you some nights, sleeping beside her, when you'd feel unable to close your eyes for fear of its darkness. Maybe you feared what the darkness would reveal in you. You didn't consider that the dark could be what holds you, as much as you hold it. Or maybe you did.

You return from the conference to find your lover's things (even books) waiting in the room closest to the front door, the more efficient to move out the next day. Who put those nails in your rib cage, and how can her hammer hurt from across town? You crumple into a pile of dirty clothes and emerge a week later to vacuum underneath the bed. Her closet is empty now except for a dusty gear bag given to both of you as a wedding present. She didn't want to take the blackout curtain either. You close the doors. All of the doors are closed.

Someone once told you that there is no safe space.

The body closet is voracious. It wants to take up space but is only so big. It wants to shout even if it has no voice. It wants kung pao chicken. It wants General Tso's and beef broccoli, too. It wants hand-pulled and vermicelli noodles. It wants broth so thick with bone it is chewy. It wants a daikon dildo and fortune cookie pasties. It wants a cake orgy. It wants cheese and carbs suffocating every orifice. It wants to run over to the ramen aisle and dump every package of instant noodles into the cart, fearing and living for that moment you look into the cashier's face.

I wish these walls could protect us. I wish my walls could provide you safety. I wish I could heal myself.

You blur on the dance floor, so open and silent as you mouth-shout the lyrics. You can only dance thinking no one knows you and no one will ask you to speak. You sweat, becoming sauna, becoming warped wood.

I sit and watch Project Runway with my mother because Tim Gunn is our spirit animal, if our relationship had a spirit animal. We make it work and don't speak of our asexuality. I picture the iridescent stretch marks along her stomach I'd see in the bathroom growing up, her hefty hands grabbing the loose skin saying, this is from you and your sister. I liked the stretch marks because they resembled mermaid skin: that look of light dancing, of being a creature of sun and water. I wanted to know I came from something a little fantastic. I remember feeling for her breast as a child, too old then to be sleeping with my mother, turning toward her as she read her library romance novels on that futon in an upstairs bedroom at my grandparents', the one with a mirror sliding door and a box television where I'd watch TGIF on ABC. One night I woke up with a nosebleed, but I couldn't be sure because of the floral sheet pattern. What was I feeling for?

I can't get too close; it feels like a secret I should keep forever. Who would understand? And I wouldn't want someone to understand something about my life that I do not. Don't tell me. Don't tell me what you think. I don't want to judge it and I don't want judgment. It's just there, part of it all. Barely there if you ignore it. Don't look at it too closely because I'm not there yet. Please don't talk to me about this. Store it away.

T wants to know if dating a lesbian says something about them. Is their gender compromised by agreeing to a first date? I feel so Asian then, thinking of how I need to shout LESBIAN so people take my fluid, long-haired self seriously. Lesbian means fuck you patriarchy, fuck you colonialism,—and please, please fuck me as I want, however abject or uneventful. The I word doesn't fit right, but what has? This body, too boxy and so tiny. Too tense and never tight enough. Work with it, though. As if I grew up with Merle Woo in my ear or Kitty Tsui's spiky hair in my mind. Now I know they were in the air of the world I breathed toward, and somehow I'm breathing, too. Now I know I was never becoming alone. The journey to now has been full of swishy gays parting the sweat of street crowds for me, older queers laying out a glitter path like a fairy tale witch, lezzies writing in seclusion and creating family with plants and three- and four-legged life. I always wanted something to convert to, and then José pointed me to the bathroom. (My anxious bladder is a story for another time.) I didn't get to ask him: what if your body is the horizon line?

You are a closet with doors that lead to other worlds, like a wardrobe with a trail of apricot lokum or sour plum. You do not yet know the worlds your closet holds. They will astound you, thrill you, bring you to your knees. But they will hold you, for they are your body and they are your self, for you are that closet that is that world of worlds.

WOVEN MOMENTS

Su-An Ng

Title: Woven Moments
Duration: 10 minutes

Directed and Animated by Su-An Ng
Produced by Beatrice Chew
Original Music and Sound Design by Claudine Michael
Animation assistants: Beatrice Chew, Claudine Michael, William Nghiem
In collaboration with artist Michele Morcos
Commissioned by Transport for NSW

"Woven Moments" is an abstract expressionistic animation reflecting on our interconnectedness to each other, the land we live on, and the space we exist in. This work meditates on moments in time, flowing across multiple dimensions. It is inspired by the quantum physics theory that everything in the universe exists simultaneously in particle and wave states.

Blending traditional and new media, the tactile quality of "Woven Moments" brings an immersive sense of warmth to the surrounding space. This engagement of viewers through nature's movements enlivens biophilia, our innate tendency to seek connections with nature.

Moments of calm, punctuated by glimpses of atmospheric spectacle, will surprise and engage the viewer as vivid, textural elements fill the screen. Intricate particles are drawn onto painterly landscapes, creating a cinematic symphony of colour. These intricate visceral forms grow and evolve, accelerate then soften into subtle lingering forms, evoking the feeling of fleeting, ephemeral memory. Known as Heraclitean motion, it is these movements which mimic those found in nature that are associated with safety and tranquility, triggering an automated "relaxation response" in viewers.

As this work challenges screen boundaries to become part of a spatial environment, passersby are immersed, integrated, and encouraged to connect with a digital public space: a combination of suspending, compressing, and stretching resonates with the interwoven nature of space and time.

Merging the known with the unknown, this work gracefully runs parallel to the architectural theme inspired by the landscape and geology of the Sydney region. Through the journey and motion of "Woven Moments," it is our aim to help restore balance and a sense of calm in the tense and frenetic environment of a commuter pathway in the central business district. In this simulation of the layered complexity of ecosystems, our sensory systems are engaged to explore, encouraging curiosity through visual fascination.

RISE OF THE GAYSIANS: AN ORIGIN STORY

Janine Sy

I felt like the baddest bitch in the club. I was flanked by my girls (and a token straight boy). It was the *Ocean's 8* and *Crazy Rich Asians* crossover no one asked for, but everyone needed. We had flown in from all corners of the United States (really just Seattle and Washington, DC) for this very moment. It was months in the making and here we were.

To my right there was our Korean, Harvard-bound, dapper dyke and Chinese media industry futch. To my left there was our Korean LHB (long-haired butch, for the uninitiated) who only dates femmes. And then there was Greg. Greg is the only cis-het male friend the dapper dyke vacations with and was just tagging along.

Then me, a self-labeled Renaissance dyke. I am a Chinese (by way of the Philippines) dyke of all traits (realistically, equal part sports and industry dyke, with many attempts at being an arts femme) who still gets hit on by cis-het men. After the last wrist had been stamped, we looked at each other, went in for a group hug, took in a collective breath, and walked in. I absolutely felt like Beyoncé backstage with Destiny's Child right before the 2013 Super Bowl halftime show. This moment was sponsored by Absolut Vodka. Who are we kidding—we are not white, cis gay men. The space we have, we made for ourselves.

Six months before that glorious moment, a wise Persian sage in the form of an arts femme, self-identified "kitchen top" told me, *If you don't advocate for yourself, nobody will.* She hosts pop-up dinner parties at her apartment where strangers become friends—or at least Instagram followers. At one of these parties, dinner and discussion had already concluded, but I hung around for the leftover tahdig. Initially, our conversation revolved around her coming up in New York City during the late '80s and '90s where NYC was the gay mecca and queer culture was dictating pop culture. Then our conversation shifted to the present. At one point, Parisa asked me, *How did we get from Stonewall to millennial pink?* Her remarks in the winter of 2018 eerily foreshadowed Pride 2019, also known as the Taylor Swift concert at the Stonewall Inn. In response, I asked her what millennials such as myself should do to push the gay agenda forward instead of passively reaping fruit from the struggle of those before us. She replied, *Make space for yourself, because by doing that, you make space for others.* I initially felt overwhelmingly alone. The kind of alone that can be only scored by a Thom Yorke soundscape or alternately something written by Justin Vernon in the woods. With pneumonia. Fighting the stale, pale plague of veganism in the Pacific Northwest felt daunting and impossible. But at the same time, I could see my well-being contingent on the presence of a community that reflected me in more ways than one. A community that did not yet exist.

I was dating women from dating apps, perfecting "the three Fs": friend, foe, or fuck. The first two are self-explanatory, the third an all-encompassing term for any semblance of romance. It's an assessment tool I had crafted to screen my dates. In the sea of white women I had gone out with over the past few months, I went out with two Korean women. Within the first five minutes of both first dates, we were overwhelmingly in the "friend" category. With both, those dates quickly evolved past "friends" into the "homegirl" category. Each individually voiced the same sentiment of, *Where are the rest of us?* We all had friends that were queer. We had friend groups that were primarily Asian. But somehow, we had bypassed each other at this particular intersection until now.

Finally, one day I talked to a gaysian I knew from church and pitched an idea that felt so ludicrous, but so life-giving at the same time: Could I possibly assemble the next Spice Girls over a jiaozi/momo/gyoza/mandu/dumpling-making party?

The lesbiAZN council, aka the BOBAES, aka the gaysians, had our first gathering over hot pot. In attendance were my two date fails and my queer Korean friend from church. One of the date fails brought her Vietnamese friend who was getting divorced from her wife. Over the propane flame and boiling brisket, the women detailed coming out to their parents and the heartache that came with it. This was not after two drinks, or even three—this was within the first thirty minutes. Despite this, I spent the whole evening feeling like I was on my toes, trying to get a read on the other women. Did this group of strangers truly enjoy the company or were they being the socially generous, accommodating daughters our cultures had conditioned us to be? What was happening felt too good to be true. By the end of the evening, we were already planning our next get-together. I felt so seen in all my Chinese-ness and queerness because this was a space I had made for myself. This was a space that reflected me in almost every single way. This was a space I didn't have to preface any story with, "In my culture . . ." or, "When dating women . . ." All that time and energy that would have been expended giving explanations was spent on meaningful conversation instead.

The *L Word* and *Joy Luck Club* remix had arrived. The conversations, the way love and affection were expressed, and our shared courtesies also made me feel seen. Within the first two dinners we had already walked through a divorce, a breakup of a relationship of eight years, and coming out to religious parents. Love is expressed in the form of serving cut-up fruit (with a preference for citrus especially), mirroring the love we have received from our grandmothers, mothers, and aunties. Affection is also expressed in the, *Don't you dare try to pay and insult me, I'll beat your ass,* when the bill comes out. People almost never show up empty-handed to dinner. After dinners, we all observe the unspoken courtesy that everyone helps the host clean up.

There was a night we went to a club for an event that centered people of color and the LGBT+ community. I hesitated to walk in because I had a fleeting but very paralyzing moment of fear that I would run into my ex, since that was also a space she occupied. One of the lesbiAZNs turned around and caught me balking at the entrance, unable to step in. She looked at me with a touching degree of kindness and sincerity, and said, *Never leave a space because of someone else. It's your space and you belong here too.* My experiences felt validated within the group, but also so seen by the rest of the world because of my girls. There have been numerous times among friends and dates that have said, "Invite the Council, we'd love to see you all there." I was no longer the token queer or Asian; instead, we were there together in solidarity. We walk into restaurants, clubs, tea bars, and concerts as a gaggle of unapologetic gaysians. There is no greater satisfaction than watching heads turn and eyes linger.

Sometimes, new members are added to our ranks. Typically, we introduce ourselves with our astrological and Asian zodiac signs. Libra, year of the rooster. Dragon, Scorpio but Sagittarius cusp. Year of the horse, Gemini (always met with a collective eye roll)! Conversation is absolutely always over food. Works such as *The Handmaiden* (especially the Power Ranger sex scene) and *Saving Face* consistently get brought up. After all, the Asian lesbian canon is only two movies deep, until Alice Wu finishes *The Half of It*. Then there will be three and more to discuss! Get-togethers often end with all of us piling into cars, zooming towards boba or bingsoo, and talking until the establishment kicks us out.

As we entered that club, I wish I could say that hordes of beautiful women flocked to us with Mary J. Blige's "Just Fine" blaring in the background. Or even that the whole club stared and admired our beauty as we walked into Mariah Carey's "Fantasy." Instead, we made our way to the bar only to be asked to leave as they were doing CPR on an unresponsive person on the dance floor. We then found ourselves down the block at Flaming Saddles, a Wild West–themed gay bar with strippers pole-dancing, dressed in cowboy garb. Despite the hilarity of our surroundings, we danced the night away, got drunk, got high, made a spontaneous pit stop at the "lamps" outside of LACMA (Los Angeles County Museum of Art), and ordered McDonald's from UberEats at 3 a.m. I absolutely felt like Emma Watson in that one tunnel scene in *The Perks of Being a Wallflower*. The possibilities of these friendships felt (and still feel) endless. In this community I feel a sense of groundedness from simply knowing they get it. If anything, our solidarity in comparing notes on whose ex is prowling Bumble and who else to not date via the dating apps has been useful. And best of all, I can walk through life reassured that there is a community out there that will change out of their pajamas, put on their pants, and grab bubble tea with me.

MONOCHROME

Meghna Chatterjee

incandescent
under the slowly turning
morning, your skin shines
with the brave glow of one with no
consciousnesses of self,
soft pink in the jarring vibrance
of the Indian bustle. How
carefully you assume your place
in the picture, with your boys around you,
hand on hips,
and new age binary clothes, subtly
yet conspicuously aware
that your softest whisper
will drown my loudest cry
without the simplest challenge
in my monochrome country,
that lives and breathes in denial
of its own beauty;
gently lingering, I can see the gentle pride
in your eyes.

AFTERNOON REVERIE

Meghna Chatterjee

At noon we fall asleep in distant places
treading on dreams in quiet toes,
I can see you, mountain at moondawn—
like a watchman in the sky, pallid, unreaching.

Months fly by like carriages in trains, whistles echoing
a hundred billion many windows for watching space—
I am a stargazer finding constellations in the summer sky.

We wear our memories like Lego pieces in our pockets, open edges,
I'll stack them together to make a fence around us—build us a
                                        garden, and
leave your poetry in the soil.
I'll unwind like a rose within your arms; keep me pressed within
                                        your pages,
for even flowers grow old and die

eyelids flicker; a whisper; two bodies in the dark.
the garden you've grown in the space between us
is filled with poetry with nowhere to go.
I no longer belong to myself—
        I can hear my name ricochet between your ribs.

LOVE LETTERS TO TOSHI

Syd Westley

I.

When the light breaks, how does it feel against the skin of your body? When it rains, which hat do you wear and do you think of me when you do? It's been one hundred sixty days since I saw you, and the Earth hasn't even slowed down. There have been a great many fires which burned down the mountains, and then a rain which hasn't stopped in many months. O Toshi, it has been raining in Marin too. I have kissed a girl often and collected the rainwater in the back of her throat. There are so many words I have to give you, and so many words that I can't. I think of mom and the way that she held your hand each weekend the way I hold a girl's hand in the mornings. There is a softness in that, one that I learned from walking with you. There is a boy in me, one that I am trying to find the words to bring out. If only you had had more time, I think you would have liked him too. He keeps me company on the nights when I can't help but picture your smile. I am not lonely anymore. How do I tell you that without you I feel so much more alive?

II.

Nana, some things hold me better than others and when you left, I turned to Esther, the Earth. She holds me too, in her hands late at night. As is light, there is soil, and I feel her in my palms and dig and dig and dig. I wish you could hear the wind's soft whistle. I wish you could know the slight bend of the trees at my touch, the feel of the stones beneath my feet.

III.

That a body could hold it all.
That a death could overflow.

A granddaughter becomes a grandson.
I am the same child, the same child.

I say you do not reject me from heaven.
I say there is no world in which we do not inherit
each other.

SNAPSHOT LESBIAN LOVE CELEBRATION
Dolphin Waletzky

In 1975, someone asked me if I was a lesbian. "Why?" I said. "Because these events are coming up for Bimillennial Lesbian Week [in Western Massachusetts], but you need to be a lesbian to go to them." "Oh, yeah. I'm a lesbian!" So I went to the weekend retreat in the hills, and, although I'm not usually a workshop fan, I saw one called "Lesbian Visions," given by Elana. I was so excited and happy! Someone's talking about visions in a political/spiritual context! These are my people, my family. Then Elana gave a poetry reading, and I thought – if she ever knew me, we would be great friends.

In 1978, many of us left the Northampton area for points west. I was traveling with a friend and we pulled up to the Pagoda in Saint Augustine, Florida (a famous lesbian landmark in those days) when we heard someone call, "Ambrose!" "I know a dog named Ambrose," my friend said. "Oh – and I know Elana!" – and there she was. Later I found Elana on the beach. I pulled everything out of the pocket of my white pants – those were the days we carried crystals and shells everywhere – and said, "Take anything."

Within a week, we had left the Pagoda and started caravanning around the South together with two dogs, a breadtruck made into an RV, a car, and three Jewish dykes. Elana and I ended up in Oregon, came to Oakland after four years, and then Elana dumped me in 1986. We had a couple rough years, and then gradually couldn't resist each other's unique presence in our lives.

We've evolved into – into whatever the word is that doesn't exist yet – for intergalactic intimacy. We've gone on dozens of road trips over the decades, taken care of each other's pets, been good friends with each other's mothers, comforted each other through losses, shown up at emergency rooms, been a harbor for each other in the most difficult times, shared many meals and laughter.

Elana and I are cozy comfort. As Elana would say, "For as long as it's good." And I say, "Forever."

Elana Dykewomon

In the early 70s, I was busy being an activist and by 1975, engaging in all the internecine arguments that now seem typical of young movements (or young people in movements). So the first time I was aware of Dolphin was when she stood before me on that St. Augustine beach, offering me whatever stone or bead I wanted from her pockets. We watched TV on the tiny b&w set I had hooked up in the RV (a shop teacher's homemade version), and managed to become lovers on its unstable narrow beds.

We were happy. The story of our travels, of our life on the Southern Oregon coast, our coming apart and coming back together could fill a book – which I have been trying to write for awhile. She became the best critic of my writing, detailed and precise. In our first incarnation, I called her "the athlete of dawn" (when she woke me at five to watch sunrise over the Florida marshes) and "the angel of decadence" (when she ate three flans in a row when we went to Puerto Rico to visit my mother).

Even when she was most mad at me for "dumping her" – her version, not mine (though I admit to an extremely ungraceful exit from cohabiting partnership) – we were always deeply involved with each other's energies. What I value most in my intimacies is the steadfastness to stay engaged, to see each other through. We both had other partners and loves over these forty-two years, but we've always lived within five miles of each other and shown up – both for difficulties and pleasures.

When my twenty-seven-year partnership with my spouse, Susan Levinkind, ended with Susan's death in 2016, Dolphin stayed with me for weeks, sleeping on my couch, walking my dog, giving me both room to grieve and a witness. She's slept on my couch almost every Friday night since then – my pandemic pal, my life-long friend. My Dolphin – among the most satisfying words I know.

BOOK REVIEWS

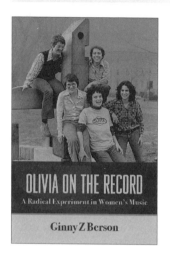

Olivia on the Record: A Radical Experiment in Women's Music
by **Ginny Z Berson**
Aunt Lute Books, San Francisco, 2020;
paperback $19.95

Reviewed by Roberta Arnold

In *Olivia on the Record*, Ginny Berson shares with us a chronicle of Olivia Records: stories in a time when women who declared themselves lesbian feminist shared a familiar bond of politics and living to include "giving voice to women's different realities, providing opportunities for women to learn and practice new skills and then create networks among themselves, building community...." (16). Berson's clear insight, drive, indomitable spirit, and open-heartedness are gifts that put the book and Olivia Records in the forefront of things we can learn from.

The book is impeccably documented, from files Berson kept, with personal details and quoted materials so vivid one might imagine a time much more recent than 70 years ago. The book begins in 1956, when Berson's dream to be a Yankees ballplayer is upended. This lesson marked the beginning of Berson's drive to right the tilted playing field; inequality was personal to her. In 1970, she joined the Furies, in DC, with other lesbian feminist separatists, including Rita Mae Brown, Coletta Reid, and Charlotte Bunch among them. The Furies had a systematic work ethic approach to political activism that including theory as well as publication of a newsletter that would spread the ideological thoughts they believed in. Berson breaks them down into 6 core beliefs the first of which is this, "Sexism is the root of all oppressions. Lesbian and woman oppression will not end by smashing capitalism, racism, imperialism, and all other forms of domination. Sexism is not the bad behavior of some men; it is a system of oppression that operates on a personal level as well as on an institutional and structural level." (p 38) This is just the first chapter. It carefully lays out the beginnings of Berson's ascent to lesbian feminist principles with the title, "The Road I Took: *I Could Have Been a Yankee but Instead I Became a Fury*" (17). On the paperback cover is a photo by JEB, who was also a member of The Furies. The photo features the Olivia Records Collective during the early years, "The Olives," as they called themselves, Jennifer Woodul, Meg Christian, Ginny Berson, Kate Winter, and Judy Dlugacz. The collective would expand by the summer of 1977 to include the musician composer arranger, Mary Watkins, composer of the opera *Dark Matters: The Fannie Lou Hamer Story* (2009), Linda Tillery who produced and sang with the BeBe K'Roche band on the album Olivia made in 1976, and a second solo Olivia album in 1977. Michelle Clinton, an African American poet also joined the collective that summer. Olivia also brought two white working class women into the collective, Sandy Ramsey and the musician Teresa Trull, whose first solo album came out with Olivia in 1977.

In 1973, the launch of Olivia Records began as the combination of many dreams, dreams that would effectively change the world, as well as the music industry, for the better. Olivia sprouted organically, in keeping with the spontaneity of the time. Berson and Meg Christian, the singer songwriter, had begun a romantic relationship. Meg Christian and Cris Williamson had met and sung together; both were struggling with making music in a world that depreciated lesbian feminist principles. In a feminist radio collective interview, Williamson unloads her frustration at having no control of the music making process. Afterwards, Williamson suggests to Berson and Christian, "Why don't you start a women's record company?" To which Berson responds affirmatively. "And that was it. I knew immediately what I was going to do. I did not have one second of doubt" (68).

One of the records Olivia Records released was a record of Judy Grahn reading with Pat Parker. The LP, recorded in 1976, *Where Would I Be Without You: The Poetry of Pat Parker & Judy Grahn*, was recorded in the living room of Sandy Stone, sound engineer in the Olivia Records Collective. Stone was a transwoman introduced to the collective by other sound engineers for her skills and prowess in the field, having worked with Hendrix, and with Van Morrison on *Tupelo Honey*. Stone got so much flak from the lesbian community, she eventually left, and has since authored the essay, "The Empire Strikes Back: a Posttranssexual Manifesto." Berson and Olivia Records continued to support Stone and their decision to include her, insisting that someone who gives up their privilege of being a man to identify as a lesbian who embraces feminist principles would always be a welcome part of their community. In *Olivia on the Record*, Berson does not sugarcoat or downplay the backlash and vitriol of the lesbian feminist separatist community.

Notable joys and storms meld nevertheless. Through Berson's recounting, the stories thread together seamlessly as sewed quilt pieces. The visions and dreams realized by Olivia Records were a clarion call of second wave lesbian feminists who believed in doing something to change inequality, building a strong hearthstone in the homes of those denied a safe haven. Olivia Records believed they could change history – and they did. This drumbeat resounds through *Olivia on the Record* with an intensity similar to the recorded voices of Olivia Records.

One of the historical records Berson revives is from the acclaimed *Lesbian Concentrate* cover album. This was recorded at a time when the fight against homosexuality was at an all-time high, led by Anita Bryant in Florida. The parallel to today is spine chilling. But it was still a more dangerous time to be a lesbian in the 60s and 70s overall. Berson tells us how in 1977 you could lose your apartment, your children, your job, be committed to a mental institution, and be raped as punishment (197). Berson continues to explain how anti-discrimination ordinances that had begun in cities across the nation were pounced upon by people such as Anita Bryant in Miami. In her campaign, "Save the Children," religious liberty juxtaposed with images of sex abuse was used as a trope to attack homosexuality and illicit fear (198). The scare tactics sounding much like the scare tactics of the religious right today that falsely accuse Democrats of child trafficking. Berson ends this history lesson on a trenchant up note, "For the most part, none of the attacks even acknowledged the existence of lesbians. We were, after all, just women, and besides, nobody could figure out what lesbians did in bed---how was it possible to have sex without a penis involved?" (199).

The *Lesbian Concentrate* album's crowning glory was its embrace of the landscape of women loving women along with its famous insert. From inside the covers of this iconic LP was a statement from Olivia Records, titled, "Out to Change the World!" Berson gives us this taste:

> What is a lesbian, a lesbian is a woman who loves women, who counts on women for her emotional support, who looks to women for her growth, who finds her identity in her womanhood. A lesbian is a woman who, more and more willingly, and with more and more pride, knows and shows her strength, makes her own definition for herself, and dares to defy society's most sacred taboo---"Thou shalt not live without men and like it!" (206)

Each chapter in *Olivia on the Record* is a clear smooth transition from one to the next and the writing flows seamlessly. Berson credits Aunt Lute Books for helping with the editing process, along with crediting the women still alive from the 70s who helped by remembered stories from so long ago. Berson brings in Julie Enszer & Cheryl Clarke who remind us of the time gone by:

> Forty years after the release of *Where Would I be Without You*, a generation of young people do not know what record albums are. Phonographs, album covers, A side and B side, record sleeves, and liner notes are things from the past. (195)

Berson's memory and file keeping is most admirable in every step of Olivia's journey, including unveiling personal heartbreak and joy. She tell us, "For me, more than anything---other than Meg's *I know You Know*---*Where Would I Be Without You* was a project of my heart. This record represented the essence of why

I wanted to start a women's record company in the first place. As Judy (Grahn) said about women's poetry, from "Anathema,' which we printed on the back of the album jacket:

> art is not a way out, there is no way out.
> there is only what we've got and how to turn it
> around to reinforce our fighting genius; to
> clarify and point out what has been stolen
> from us and that we must take it back or continue
> with nothing.
> at its best it comes from our bitterest anger,
> our most expansive love, our most courageous
> hopes, our most vital visions, our most honest
> insights, our fiercest determination (196).

Olivia on the Record is a beautiful gift, a rare treasure. My sister uncovered 4 LPs by Olivia Records after my mother died and although we could no longer play them, we recognized them for the invaluable gifts that they are. Passed down from the pioneering gale makers of the second wave steering us to where we are now, these voices are our heritage. Similarly, in *Olivia on the Record,* Berson passes down to us much more than the inaccessible artifacts of vinyl records as she recreates the vision, inspiration, stories and lessons lived. The collective of Olives changed the tides, pulling the second wave forward. Olivia Records truly moved the markers too, and justices begun by their pushcart have now dropped off for us this important gift, unearthed and revivified treasure by Ginny Berson.

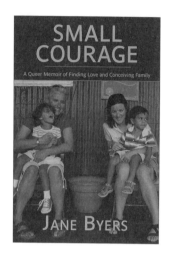

Small Courage: A Queer Memoir of Finding Love and Conceiving Family
by **Jane Byers**
Caitlin Press, 2020
Paperback, 192 pages, 24.95

Reviewed by Juno Stilley

"It is a privilege to witness another's life," Jane Byers writes in her book *Small Courage: A Queer Memoir of Finding Love and Conceiving Family*. This book offers readers exactly that - the privilege to experience Byer's life as she tells it: dotted with many moments of small courage, as well as heaps of big courage. Byers uses a nonlinear timeline of her life to weave pain, joy, childhood, and parenthood together. She divulges her experience traversing the Canadian adoption process and embarking on parenting a set of twins with her wife, Amy. She writes about her complex relationships with her own parents and siblings and how many of her adolescent experiences inform her own parenting now. On the surface, *Small Courage* is about queer parenthood. Looking deeper, this memoir explores how both love and trauma can transform the individual.

Byers brings readers along for the entire process of 'conceiving family,' as she puts it; from a momentous camping expedition where the couple decide they want to have children, to finally bringing home their baby twins, Franny and Theo. It is with joy seeping through the page that Byers writes of being confirmed as the official guardians of the twins, saying "We cried and danced around the condo, each of us with an oblivious toddler in our arms. 'We are a forever family!' we exclaimed." Byers also details the numerous and often homophobic obstacles faced throughout the adoption process. The twins are fostered by an Evangelical Christian couple, with whom Byers and Amy have a nuanced and surprising relationship. With strength, Byers and Amy push through the endless paperwork and questions. Byers succeeds in detailing not only the adoption process and her other adventures through life in a multi-dimensional way, but the entire world as a mosaic. At every opportunity, Byers graces her readers with understanding of systems in place, beliefs, and actions of others.

Byers writes big ideas simply. She rarely dives deeply into description, instead focusing on dialogue and the senses. She retells memories in a 'cause-and-effect' style, where she often explains first what happened, and then what it taught her in the long run. That same simplistic writing style still expresses brave vulnerability and is deeply effective. She manages to reveal a lot in less than 200 pages. Throughout the memoir, there is some repetition. Stories are repeated briefly and readers are taken back to places in Byers' life they have already been, with seemingly nothing added. This may have been a conscious choice in order to keep readers in context, as each chapter is jumping from very different parts of her life.

Small Courage is written with care. Byers explains her experience being a white parent with mixed children ("South Asian and likely Caucasian"), with deliberate notice of her challenges and the racism the children face. Her own childhood trauma is handled with love for herself. Even when briefly speaking on her family's experiences throughout Covid-19, Byers works through it on the page. The natural outdoors, which is the setting for many of Byers' most paramount moments, is expressed with inspiring grandeur and respect. She shows readers she loves the Earth clearly, without needing to explicitly state as much. This love of life is clear on the page.

Byers writes with great command and pacing in her work. Final sentences of paragraphs often yield a reward to readers with their gravity. Byers knocks the air right out of readers. Original poems dotted throughout are purposely placed, written at the time of the events that are described in the chapter and work as a revelatory, lyrical perspective of the same experience she just shared. Byers is clearly a literary lover and aficionado, with references to other works seamlessly placed throughout the book. These reasons, among others, make Byers' writing exciting to read.

Small Courage is full of big wisdoms. Byers teaches readers about healing and communication. She works through growing up and the ever changing relationship with family and with oneself. The slew of parenting advice, told from the perspective of mistakes made and learning curves overcome, demands much underlining. This book seems like it would be most treasured in the hands of a parent-to-be. But Byers has profound ideas for readers in all periods of their lives. She says: "To love is to see and not try to change." This is an extremely important insight, something that Byers had to learn through experience but gives to readers as a gift.

While this memoir is written with much more life still to be lived, Byers' is able to give readers a lot to think about. With an ideal amount of glances to the past and the future, this book feels like getting to know someone from all the lessons they have learned. Readers witness who Byers is from what she has been through, and there is space left for what she will continue to discover. Throughout, readers can feel how much Amy and Jane love each other and their children. Byers includes her final sentence of her wedding vows to Amy: "Above all, I will see you, with my eyes and heart as open as I am able." Byers writes her own memoir of "finding love and conceiving family" with the same openness. For that powerful truth alone, *Small Courage* is well worth a read. Thank you Jane Byers for the privilege of witnessing your life thus far.

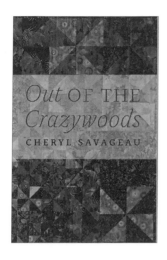

Out of the Crazywoods
by **Cheryl Savageau**
University of Nebraska Press, 2020
Cloth, 264 pages, 29.95

Reviewed by Kim Shuck

I have been sitting at my computer since 4am and it's now 6:30. It is November of 2020, the days when the election results are still being evaluated. I've had

Out of the Crazywoods for a few months now. I've read it all the way through several times. I've read pieces of it. It's hard to know what's going to happen in the world because of Covid-19, a President I can't begin to characterize, and unprecedented social stratification. If you are not Indigenous you should probably also know that, for us, those shared crises have landed on the ongoing crisis that is colonization, marginalization, and racism. Why would you or I want to read a book about someone else's psychological challenges in this of all moments? Maybe this is why it took me so long to review?

Cheryl Savageau and I are connected by friends, the kind of friends who would lay down in traffic for you. We are both Indigenous women of a certain age, meaning we will say uncomfortable things at random moments because we're not here to make you feel comfortable.

Out of the Crazywoods is a memoir. Savageau is a brilliant writer. I read her work. I've taught her work. I've bought her books at full price in the month they have been released. I read her, not to be entertained, but so that I feel more real. I read Cheryl because independence is getting rid of a mouse infestation, because I don't play well with others either, because I take her work personally.

Within the book, I recognized moments when teachers, in her case a nun, have explained that a comment was not appropriate for class, that some concerns are outside of the curriculum. *Out of the Crazywoods* is not about misunderstood genius, malicious narcissism, or dank psychiatric hospitals full of moans and body fluids. This book is about not being able to keep a job. It's about the daily heroic adventure of living. There is mouse poo, but there is also magnificence.

If you are an Indigenous woman you need to read this book. You should also read this book if you have been inundated with stereotypes about Indigenous women, mental illness, or have been subject to relentless sexism. I read obsessively, have done since I was seven years old. I read science, all kinds of fiction, history, signs on the public transit, the plastic emergency cards on airplanes. This book took time and I'm really good at books. *Out of the Crazywoods* falls outside of the curriculum, it's not easy, and you should read it.

OBITUARY

Remembering Lenn Keller
(September 29, 1950 - December 16, 2020)

by Rebecca Silverstein

Self-Portrait by Lenn Keller

Lenn was a generous, beautiful, fierce, brilliant woman, a Black gender non-conforming lesbian, who worked tirelessly for decades collecting materials and documenting, through her photos and films, the culture of lesbians, especially Black lesbians and lesbians of color, in the San Francisco Bay Area.

She was the founder of the Bay Area Lesbian Archives, which has one of—if not the largest—collection percentage-wise of lesbians of colors materials as well as other marginalized communities within the lesbian community.

She was also my best friend, family, mentor, and co-partner in the archives.

Her sudden passing, from a stage 4 cancer diagnosis in late October, is hitting the Bay Area hard. We are mourning her loss deeply.

***

In *Sinister Wisdom* 71, published in the summer of 2007, Lenn Keller contributed the essay, "Welcome to the 21st Century: A Feminist Butch Is Not an Oxymoron." Keller concluded the essay:

Being so much more my authentic self today, owning my butchness is exhilarating and empowering. Claiming my butchness, honoring and acknowledging it, I feel more attractive than

I've ever felt in my whole life. I love being butch for a femme who appreciates it, wats it—gets it. Thankfully, I finally did figure out that I am butch, and that to be a butch and a feminist is not an oxymoron—that I can be in a butch/femme relationship that is not sexist, misogynist or homophobic. I fully accept myself now as the femme loving butch that I've always been. It's great to be alive in the 21st century.

Sinister Wisdom appreciates Lenn Keller's many contributions and joins the community of care in remembering her and her work.

"Self-Portrait #5" © H. Lenn Keller

Donations may be made in Lenn Keller's memory to the Bay Area Lesbian Archive.

Please make out your check payable to Bay Area Lesbian Archives and mail it to: BALA Inc., PO Box 3494, Oakland, CA 94609.

Remembering Kim Chernin:
Writer, Editor, Quester, Visionary, Friend
by Lise Weil

Kim Chernin died on December 17, after two strokes and a fall which landed her in rehab. There, at the age of 80, she contracted COVID. It is very hard to take in that Kim is no longer with us. I think that is because when she was with us she was SO with us. It's what made her writing, on any subject, so compelling. I could always feel her there—completely—wherever she took me. And as an eternal quester she took us to some far-flung places: an Israeli border kibbutz (*Crossing the Border*), a small town in Germany to interview Italian opera singer Cecilia Bartoli (*Cecilia Bartoli: The Passion of Song*), yet another obscure German village to sit *darshan* with Hindu teacher Mother Meera (*In My Father's Garden*). Mostly, though, the journeys were interior ones: into the mysteries of women and food (*The Obsession: The Tyranny of Slenderness, The Hungry Self, Reinventing Eve: Modern Woman in Search of Herself*), into the mysteries of mother-daughter relationships (*In My Mother's House, The Flame Bearers, The Woman Who Gave Birth to Her Mother*), into the mysteries of sex and gender and desire (*Crossing the Border, My Life as Boy* and *Sex and Other Sacred Games*, co-authored with her partner Renate Stendhal).

I got to know Kim and Renate in 1991 after writing a long review of *Sex and Other Sacred Games* for *Trivia: A Journal of Ideas* of which I was then editor. An extended conversation between two women on the subject of sex in the course of which they fall in love, the book was a revelation to me. I had never seen sex and desire explored with such audacity and complexity: two women unmasking their own and each other's deepest fears and desires. Renate and Kim each wrote a short text to accompany my review and a friendship began to develop—but initially only with Renate. Kim was a hermit, Renate explained. But many years later, decades in fact, and only once I made a pilgrimage to their home in Point Reyes, Kim came out of hiding. She was so exactly the Kim of her books I felt I had known her forever. Except she was funnier, more childlike. Compulsively honest, she had a way of making you want to deliver yourself of your darkest secrets—something that should not have surprised me in the co-author of *Sex and Other Sacred Games*.

In preparation for writing this piece I stacked up all the Chernin books I've collected over the years. It was a very tall pile. I started paging through some of them. Had imagined a kind of flyover, touching down just to recall the flavor and the theme and to see if I could pick up on common threads. But I was unable to "page through." I wanted to *read* every page. And I indulged this desire. I began rereading books I hadn't touched in almost 30 years.

Was back inside them again. Back inside... Kim... passionate brilliant mysterious sometimes hilarious Kim. Amazingly, not for a moment did I feel I was regressing—oh yes *that*—or did I read with anything less than present-moment absorption. Every page could have been written today. In many ways it seems to me we are only now catching up with the understandings in her trilogy about food and eating disorders. (*Reinventing Eve* undid me when I first read it in 1989). And with her understandings about gender: in *My Life as a Boy*, a memoir, Kim finds she can only act on her desire for the woman she has fallen in love with by physically taking on the attributes of a boy.

But I want to talk about a piece of writing by Kim that has probably not been widely read. I myself had almost forgotten about it; it was not among the volumes stacked up beside my reading chair. That's because it's a short story, collected in *Lesbian Love Stories* (edited by Irene Zahava in 1989). "An American in Paris" is not really fictional; it's an account of the three days in Paris during which Kim became lovers with Renate, the woman with whom she would spend the rest of her life. Almost shocking that I did not immediately think of this story, since reading it over thirty years ago I remember being shaken to the core. Never had I read anything that so minutely so expertly so fearlessly captured every nuance of the terror and vulnerability, the freefall, of moving toward the woman you have fallen in love with when you have absolutely no certainty regarding *her* desire: "There is an infinity of silence; more than enough in which to die of shame."

I picked up the story and read it again. Felt it all over again, this time more intensely, having acquired additional experience of my own in this realm in the years since. The vulnerability was almost unbearable. I cringed. Marvelled at Kim's skill and again her honesty as a writer. What made this scene so unlike any other love scene I've read? Apart from the writer's ability to evoke the subtlest movements of mind and body? It's because—I realize now—falling in love in this instance meant feeling all of her past lovers with her as she fell, "I have brought into this room my mother, every woman I have ever wanted and feared to love," meant shedding all armour all pretense all protection and finally, "shaking in the naked revelation of self," being utterly seen.

In retrospect I see that this driving urge to know and be known, to see and be seen, is at least implicitly present in everything Kim wrote. (It's explicit, often comically so, in *Lesbian Marriage: A Love & Sex Forever Kit*, the book she and Renate put out in 2014, the year they married, a tongue-in-cheek "advice kit" for newly married lesbians that draws on their then twenty-eight year relationship.) Kim was all about stripping away fakeness pretences subterfuge of any kind. No doubt this is why in later years she shunned publicity and sent her writings of the last decade directly to her archives. She had no interest in the business of self-promotion and marketing expected of writers today. A loss for her readers to be sure.

In Kim's writing life, this urge to know and be known was almost exclusively applied to relationships between women. In *My Life as a Boy* she wrote: "I wonder if anyone will ever tell all there is to be told about women. Women who are married, or mothers, or who meet for the first time as grandmothers often mean more to each other than anyone has ever meant to either one of them—yes, even more than husbands and children. But this truth tends to be kept a collective secret... What goes on in every moment women are alone together is taking place beyond what is culturally named and acknowledged. Because it is subtle, silent, undefined and enjoys its secrecy, the true nature of women's relationships is often kept hidden, even from women themselves." Dedicated as she was to unearthing the secrets of the body, its appetites and longings, Kim did as much as any other writer I can think of to bring that true nature to light.

I think it's important to note that in Kim's case those relationships included an ongoing bond with the Great Mother, who figures importantly in her work, most especially in *Reinventing*

Eve and her novel *The Flame Bearers*, about a sect of women in Israel devoted to Her teachings. A more recent example is "Mother of Us: A Prayer for Healing," a remarkable poetic prose piece that reads as if channeled, which I published in 2018 in *Dark Matter: Women Witnessing.*

I can't close without mentioning the great gift Kim brought to so many writers, including me, when she turned her skills and perceptions to editing the work of others. In late 2015, after countless rejections from agents and publishers, I was almost ready to give up on my memoir, which I'd been working on for twelve years. Kim had mentioned her passion for editing on my last visit. Well, I figured, my memoir is about desire. It's about relationships between women. And it's definitely about unmasking. I made a proposal, and she was in right away. Of course, I was thrilled. I was also terrified. And what I got was exactly what I most feared, and desired: that drive for truth, for unveiling, now applied to my own writing. Kim challenged me when motives seemed obscure, when I wasn't going deep enough, and also—predictably—when I and my physical world needed to be more present: "I want to be able to *feel* this," she would say. "Bring me there." But maybe most important of all, she encouraged me at a moment when I sorely needed it. The years of rejections had detached me from my book and instilled profound self-doubt. Kim's enthusiasm rallied me. In her letters she kept insisting how much she loved the book, that parts of it consistently moved her to tears. Her insightful, incisive edits would arrive with subject lines like "so wonderful." Eventually I believed her. *In Search of Pure Lust* was published in 2018, a very different and infinitely better book than the one that would have appeared without her intervention.

As the daughter of Marxist parents and a Communist organizer mother who spent her days agitating for immigrants and the poor and was at one point arrested for attempting to overthrow the US government, Kim always seemed to be measuring her own work as a writer and therapist against that of activists who were out day after day making a material difference in people's lives. It's a constant theme in the stack of books by my chair. Damn I wish I'd had a chance to lay whatever doubts she had on that score definitively to rest. To convey to Kim what seismic shifts she brought about in my life, in the lives of countless individuals, in the world: as a writer, as a lesbian, as a quester, as an editor. As a friend.

Photo credit: Claire Hope Cummings

Lise Weil was founder of *Trivia: A Journal of Ideas* (1982-1991) and its online offshoot *Trivia: Voices of Feminism* (2003-1011). Her memoir, *In Search of Pure Lust* (She Writes Press, Inanna Press, 2018) is a meditation on lesbian desire and a critical reflection on the North American women's movement of the late twentieth century. She is currently editor of *Dark Matter: Women Witnessing*, publishing writing and artwork created in response to an age of mass extinction and ecological collapse. www.darkmatterwomenwitnessing.com. She teaches in the Goddard College Graduate Institute. https://liseweil.com

María Lugones - January 26, 1944 – July 14, 2020

Marilyn Frye (left) and María Lugones (right)

A Remembrance of María Lugones

By Marilyn Frye

In the preface to *Pilgrimages/Peregrinajes* (2003) María acknowledged many dozens of essential compañeras in her theoretico-practical life's work. Groups for learning/changing were central to her intellectual and political method. In that preface she honors the Escuela Popular Norteña, Los Compañeros de las luchas en Valdez, Radical Folk at Carleton College, Methodologies of Resistant Negotiation working group at SUNY-Binghamton. I was among her conspirators in the last one she cites there, The Midwestern Division of the Society for Women in Philosophy (SWIP).

Many of us in Midwest SWIP were engaged in the radical/lesbian/anarchist wing of Second Wave feminism. In the years from early 1970s into the low '00s, Midwest SWIP met twice a year in small gatherings organized to be accessible. Women students, independent scholars, activists, and faculty philosophers gave papers, and occasionally the programs included—poetry, film, and dramatic readings. Program slots were reserved for women, and a presenter could call for a women-only audience for her paper. We provided travel grants, ride-sharing, community lodging, and lots of free food. This was the context in which I met María. María co-invented and recruited its Women of Color caucus, to which white women were not invited. María always worked in and built such contexts: inclusive-with-strategic-separations—creating and supporting multiplicitous identity and community.

It was in Midwest SWIP, before most of her works' publication, that I learned the Lugones lexicon: boomerang perception; purity/impurity; world-travelling; playfulness; mestizaje; and the rest. In this period some of us white women (just as in the women's movement at large) were in messy phases of reaching useful understanding of racism and ethnocentrism—an undertaking that was high on our shared agenda. María, brilliant and challenging, was very complexly involved with us in that practice, to which she willfully and fruitfully contributed. In those learnings and conflicts I often thought that other white women were responding to María with a performative deference that, in the context of feminist philosophical critical practice, could be recognized as disrespectful of her. And at least once, some of my colleagues perceived me as doing that.

María and I sometimes theorized together, not always in trackable ways. She took me on more directly/critically than I took her on (my deference? perhaps appropriate at some points). In our correspondence, we were working through the *Pilgrimages/Peregrinajes* essays as she revised them for the book. That process wove her thought into my own thought, into my style of thought, as no other kind of encounter could. Later, the arcs of our work diverged but we stayed in loving connection.

Marilyn Frye is the author of *Politics of Reality* and a member of *Purple*, a non-profit that established *Lesbian Legacies: Amazon Cultural/Political Activism in Second Wave Feminism* an endowment fund at the Michigan State University Library.

Remembering María Lugones

by Suparna Bhaskaran

I met María Lugones when I was a graduate student in the US Midwest at the Women of Color (WOC) Caucus at the Midwest Society for Women in Philosophy (SWIP). María was one of the cofounders of the WOC Caucus at Midwest SWIP, and referred to this space as a "freeing space" where she and other women of color could "think without the mediation of white interlocution."

I was not a student of philosophy, but María's philosophy, thinking, warmth, work, and affinity for movement building drew me to her and her world. This was the case with many other women of color in the area who were not part of the academy or philosophy departments. We/they wanted think with and be in conversation with María.

I realized very soon that I was extremely fortunate to be in her company and in the spaces that she created physically, emotionally, and intellectually. María's actions and words deepened my understanding of coalitions and how the idea of "women of color" (or being a woman of color) was fundamentally about coalitions. These coalitions meant seriously understanding our interdependence, rejecting caricatures of one another, undermining mistrust and deep divisions, and thus learning to practice deep coalitions. The Women of Color Caucus provided a space to dismantle the default impulses, generated under white supremacy, to know very little about one another and always reference our existence in relation to whiteness.

The first essay that I read by María, "Playfulness, "World"-Travelling, and Loving Perception," also allowed me as an educator to ask my students to be "responsible fools" as they sought to unlearn dominant ways of becoming radical thinkers, community members, organizers, and activists. Being foolish meant not worrying about mastery and competency and being responsible meant that learning about or speaking to oppressions (or "intermeshing oppressions") definitely was not a race. For María being in deep coalition was ultimately about our survival.

María had a visceral way of making me think about the place from where she wrote and thought (from the "dark side" or "light side") and whom she was speaking with or to. As an immigrant queer Brown woman from the Third World (living in the US) who was engaged with movement work in the Third World and in the US, María made me rethink convenient formulas of identity and adopt what she called the "art of curdling." That meant rejecting polarizing notions of race, sexuality, nationality, culture or sex/gender and the pressure to become the assimilable immigrant. She reminded me how modern categories of gender are fundamentally colonial racist creations, organized by what she called "the politics of purity."

María was an extraordinary radical Latina lesbian anarchist feminist of color who deeply influenced my worldview and ways of being. I will continue to make myself not to "think what I don't practice."

Suparna Bhaskaran is an educator and cultural worker and is currently based in Columbus, Ohio.

María Lugones, popular educator: In memoriam
by Christine (Cricket) Keating

María Lugones and I worked together for thirty years as members of the popular education collective Escuela Popular Norteña (EPN) which María founded in 1990 in northern

New Mexico. Over the years, our friendship and our work together continually challenged me to think differently and more expansively about myself and others, and deeply enlivened my sense of the possibilities of collective work.

Popular education is a mode of political praxis that grows out of critiques of hierarchical and top-down approaches to political organizing and education. It is rooted in a process of coming to critical consciousness through collective analysis and critique. In her work with the EPN and elsewhere, María developed a particularly coalitional approach to popular education, one that takes up the complexity of people's lives and communities and affirms the transformative capacity of their resistant practices. For her, our political possibilities lie in the strengthening, radicalizing, and deepening of our relationships with each other, given that our own understandings and potential enactments of our lives are inextricably tied to one another and to the meanings that we create together. This commitment to the possibility of transforming our relationships through popular education animated her work in coalition politics, in Women of Color politics, and in decolonial politics.

María very much brought a marimacha/dyke/jota sensibility to this work. A part of what she loved so much about popular education was that she could work with others to create spaces in which people practice decentering normative and hegemonic modes of being and living. For example, one EPN popular education workshop, "A Jotería: Para la Imaginación Zurda" was geared to introduce and welcome participants "to el Ambiente, el Mundo Zurdo, reality without the expectation of institutionalized heterosexuality." (El Mundo Zurdo (the left-handed world) is Gloria Anzaldúa's term. Gloria Anzaldúa, *Borderlands/La Frontera: The New* Mestiza (San Francisco: Aunt Lute Press, 2012).) As hosts, María and other members of EPN invited the participants/guests to share in imagining what is good about "la realidad vivida (the lived reality) of those of us who care/love those of our own sex"...

[in a way that is] "in intimate disrespect of the roles, movements, thoughts, relations that our communities are ordered by." María said that among the things that she most appreciated about living in el Mundo Zurdo was "having learned to love without humiliation" as well as having the freedom to experiment "with the boundaries of gender scripts." (These quotations are from the book by María Lugones and Cricket Keating, *Educating for Coalition: Popular Education and Political Praxis* forthcoming from SUNY Press.)

Given that much of what we are taught about each other in dominant society is geared to our oppression and fragmentation from each other, María believed deeply that we needed to learn about each other's lives and contexts in their complexity. Creating and crafting spaces for this learning was central to her life, whether it was in her work with communities in New Mexico or in the Andes, in her classrooms at Carleton or at Binghamton, or in tango parties at her house. In fact, just days before she died, we had a virtual meeting with community members in New Mexico to think about a popular education program for young people. She even called me from the hospital to talk about doing follow up from the meeting. She found much energy and sense of purpose in working towards the possibility of deep coalition and communality with people. I feel profoundly lucky to have been so close to her in this work and to have shared with her in this energy and purpose.

Christine (Cricket) Keating is a collective member of La Escuela Popular Norteña and teaches at the University of Washington.

Separation and Healing: Memories of María Lugones
By Crista Lebens

Fall, 2020. I am preparing to teach the essay "Purity, Impurity, and Separation." It is like visiting an old friend. This article has shaped my life and my work. Shortly after I first heard the paper presented, tragedy struck in my life when a friend committed suicide. A self-described Black Lesbian feminist and poet, she wrote, before she died, "racism is killing me." It was this essay that helped me understand better her suffering and the barriers she faced. I saw her ache for a place where she could bring all parts of herself and be welcomed. Lugones, in this essay, helped me recognize the depth of her suffering. I chose this essay for the teaching demonstration that got me my job. This is the essay that formed the basis of my dissertation and my life's work in philosophy.

On the cover of my copy of her book, *Pilgrimages/Perigrinajes*, María wrote an inscription about walking resistant paths together, yet each without losing our sense of step, but "springful," heavy and dance-like. The tensions expressed in that inscription are characteristic of the tensions that María's work encapsulates.

This essay, and Lugones' work in general has inspired students who themselves act in resistance to their own lived experience of multiple forms of oppression. Ten years later I am still in conversation with some of them about that work. They continue to interpret their lives and their conditions through that framework, and it enables them to continue.

María expressed incredible generosity toward white/anglo women such as myself who were willing to do the work. I know it cost her to be among the ones who absorbed our ignorance, our indifference, and our resistance. And yet, we had fun, too! I think of the party we threw at Midwest SWIP to celebrate the publication of *Pilgrimages/Perigrinajes*. We testified, we ate good food, we laughed, and we danced. The photo of María dancing is a bit blurry, but it conveys the joy we felt that night.

Since first encountering the essay, I have tried several times to represent visually the concepts of the unified subject, the fragmented subject, and curdled subjectivity. In graduate school as part of an independent study on Lugones' work, I created multicolored figurines one might use for a board game. Colors were split-separated in the pieces that characterized fragmentation, blended for those that represented curdled subjectivity. Later, when teaching my own class, I created images of overlapping circles with solid colors (fragmentation) and blended colors (curdling). Most recently, as I prepared to teach the essay this semester, I have drawn two-dimensional figures expressing the same distinction. This time the curdled subjects are not alone.

I am aware that Lugones created a whole new body of work on coloniality in the last decade and a half. I chose to focus on this essay from her relatively early work because I have seen the transformative effect it has had on people's lives. I believe ideas can change the world, and the ideas in this essay can even be healing. In it, Lugones has done much to help foster communities of resistance and survival.

Crista Lebens, moving continually toward curdled beingness, teaches at the University of Wisconsin-Whitewater.

CONTRIBUTORS

KIMBERLY ALIDIO is the author of *why letter ellipses* (selva oscura), : *once teeth bones coral* : (Belladonna*), *a cell of falls* (Portable Press at Yo-Yo Labs), *after projects the resound* (Black Radish), and *solitude being alien* (dancing girl press). Her prose on poetics, memory, historiography, and postcolonialism has appeared or will appear in *Harriet*, *Woodland Pattern Blog*, *Poetry Northwest*, *SocialText*, *American Quarterly*, and the essay collection *Filipino Studies: Palimpsests of Nation and Diaspora*. Her website is kimberlyalidio.com.

NAINA AYYA was born in India and raised in the US. This cosmopolitan heritage has provided her with a blend of East and West in her art that is part representational, part abstraction, and part figuration. An experienced colorist and collagist, she has a lifelong interest in exploring themes of social justice, gender fluidity, and female empowerment through her art. She resides in San Francisco.

AYIRANI BALACHANTHIRAN is an illustrator from New York whose work primarily focuses on the experience of the South Asian Queer-identified community. Their work has been featured on various platforms, including but not limited to: Indian Women's Blog, *Vatan Magazine*, The Leslie Lohman Gay and Lesbian Museum, and The People's Forum.

SAMIRAH BOOMI writes for queer Asian American women and nonbinary people who have been labeled "bad" in their families and communities. They write to reclaim their voice and story, because we aren't "bad"—we're badass. By sharing their work publicly, they hope to empower others too. You can find them on Instagram at sa.mi.ra.ni or tarotTeaPoetry, or their website at SamirahBoomi.weebly.com.

K-MING CHANG is an emerging lesbian and a Kundiman fellow. Her poetry has been anthologized in *Ink Knows No Borders*, *Best New Poets 2018*, *Bettering American Poetry Vol. 3*, and the *Pushcart Prize Anthology*. She was a Lambda Literary Award finalist in Lesbian Poetry. Her debut novel *Bestiary* is forthcoming from One World / Random House in fall 2020. Raised by matriarchs in California, she now lives in New York.
Twitter: @k_mingchang
Website: kmingchang.com

MEGHNA CHATTERJEE is a twenty-year-old writer from India, doing her graduation in English. She enjoys playing with poetic forms, loves cats, and wants to travel the world someday.

ELISHA CHEN is a junior at Cornell University, studying computer science with a minor in English. She is an ace, gay woman from San Diego, California. She enjoys writing her thoughts on personal experiences and how others might understand and relate.

CHEN XIANGYUN/谌翔云 is a queer visual artist based in Brooklyn, New York. Born and raised in Fujian, China, her work derives from being in the middle of West and East cultures, sexually, emotionally, and physically. Her art practice employs bookmaking, analog film, and photographs. She believes in making art you live more than once.

JACENNE CHLOE was discarded on the backroads of Asia, left for dead. Somehow she got lucky and was adopted by loving parents who brought her to America, where she grew into herself and found she was in love with women.

S.L. CLARKE is a human that writes. Hoping to bring forth healing and awareness through her art, she is an active advocate for women who have been victims of domestic abuse and violence.

She is the founder and editor of We Are Warriors, a community movement and publication established in 2019. Clarke writes epigrams, poetry, memoir, narratives, and song lyrics. She published her first book, *Ghost*, a poetry collection which is currently available on Amazon.

SHIVANI DAVE is a queer South Asian femme educator, artist, and lover of plants, food, magic, and rituals of healing. Her art seeks to queer what appears to be the mundane, routine, day-to-day and build connection through that exposure. She is based in NYC where she teaches full-time and writes, collages, utilizes Instagram (@getyouashiv) as a platform for self-publishing, trains in Muay Thai, and gardens, part-time. She earned her BA in biochemistry from Vassar College and her MA in teaching from Relay Graduate School of Education. She hopes to continue to work at the intersection of queerness, education, art, and biochemistry.

ABIGAIL DEL FIERRO is a poet by night and nurse by day. She can be found either in the hospital tending to the ill or meandering through a city deep in thought with a pen and notebook in hand. She aspires to write what she feels cannot be expressed openly, such as lady love. She enjoys the life in New York City.

FIONA GURTIZA is a senior editor, freelance writer, and spoken word poet. She holds a bachelor's degree in the humanities from the University of Asia and the Pacific. She aspires to teach literature or history one day. Her work has appeared in *Novice Magazine*.

JESSICA JIANG is a Chinese American lesbian illustrator. She holds a BA in ethnic studies from Brown University, and her work has been published in *Bluestockings Magazine*, the *College Hill Independent*, *Threads that Connect Us*, and *Toward A World Without Prisons*. She can be found on Twitter and Instagram at @8amtrain.

LIUXING JOHNSTON is a Chinese butch lesbian cartoonist from New Jersey. Their work focuses on the subjects of transracial adoption, Chinese American identity within the context of butch lesbian identity, the intergenerational trauma of East Asian Americans, and the emotional layers of death and the grieving process. They've spoken at the Queers and Comics Conference in 2019 and had their work published in *Butch is Not a Dirty Word* and *Lesbian Connection*. If you'd like to see more of their comics, check out their website lemonliuart.com or find them on Instagram @lemonliu32.

CRYSTAL KE Bi-racial, bi-lingual, bi-sexual, bi-cultural. Crystla Ke was born in Hong Kong and raised in Shanghai to White American and Chinese Taiwanese parents. She grew up learning traditional calligraphy but didn't have any other forms of art training ("it's a waste of time and money, it's useless"). Ever since she was young, she struggled to know my place in the world. No country would accept her as theirs, no people would accept her as theirs, and her parents' religion wouldn't accept her as theirs. But she found my voice through drawing. Black and white, ink and paper, Chinese and American, female and male. Embracing the beauty of duality to break down the idea of binaries. She has participated in two group exhibitions in Ai WeiWei's pop-up Beijing CaoChangDi space, with works focusing on misfits of traditional Chinese female pressure navigating a modern world.

JESSICA KIERAN is a proponent of dialectics, mindfulness, and self-care. As a biracial adoptee, a queer Christian, a female combat veteran, an invisible disabled person, and a mental illness fighter, Jessica works to uphold the act of striving. To strive to care. To strive to see and accept the pain of others and of oneself. To strive to scrutinize societal and personal expectations and norms. To strive to explore the active meaning of love and its relationship with the self, belief, and the world. Jessica was honored to be a judge for the 2020–21 Minnesota Book Awards. She received an Honorable Mention from the Loft's 2018–19 Mirrors and Windows Fellowship and was a 2019 Veterans' Voices Award winner. She has a BFA in writing and an MFA in writing for children and young adults from Hamline University.

SYDNEY S. KIM is a queer writer and artist based in Los Angeles. She received her MFA from the Pacific Northwest College of Art and BA from Dartmouth College. Her literary work has been published in *Wildness*, *American Literary Review*, and *Jellyfish Review*. Her visual work can be found in *Eights*, *&Review*, *Publication Studio*, and *Social Malpractice*. Her middle name is Sujin.

KAYE LIN KUPHAL is an American Chinese bisexual woman raised in the Upper South. She formerly graduated from Colgate University with a BA, having majored in biochemistry and minored in creative writing. Currently, she is attempting to establish herself as a writer and scientist and is working toward a PhD in chemistry at the University of Rochester.

SOPHIA LEE is a twenty-year-old, Korean-Italian lesbian from Brooklyn, New York. She is currently an undergraduate at Cornell University with the intent to major in linguistics and to minor in creative writing. During her senior year of high school, she won first place in the Ned Vizzini Teen Writing Contest; and most recently she was chosen to perform a spoken word poem at a school body positivity event. In her spare time, she enjoys playing guitar, writing songs, and listening to true crime podcasts to keep herself alert and prepared at all times—if not a little paranoid.

ARTEMIS LIN is a queer poet, writer, and filmmaker currently residing in Los Angeles, California. Their work is often a deep dive into their Chinese-American upbringing and explores the intersection between mental illness, trauma, dreams, memory, and family history. They have also been published in *Bright Wall/Dark Room*, *Rose Water Magazine*, and *Cha: An Asian Literary Journal*. You can follow them on Twitter @rabblerouses.

LIGHT LIU 刘亮 is a multimedia illustrator, poet, and musician based in New York. They are interested in writing experimental quantum narratives of love and loss, self and other, and absence and presence. Find more of their work at liulight.com.

VESHALINI NAIDU is a twenty-one-year-old illustrator, spoken word poet, and thespian from Malaysia.

SU-AN NG is a Canadian media artist who creates immersive moving image work inspired by nature, health, and science. She holds a bachelor of media arts, major in animation from Emily Carr University of Art and Design and was the recipient of the Emily Carr President's Media Arts Award. She is currently based in Melbourne, Australia.

JESSICA NGUYEN / NGUYỄN THỊ MAI NHI is a world traveler, activist, and writer. Though having lived in the US for most of her life, she hops from one country to the next in hopes of discovering pieces of home to fill her Vietnamese-American soul. Her prose and poetry appear in *Sinister Wisdom*, *PANK*, *diaCRITICS*, *Womanly Magazine*, and *AASIA Journal*. Her first book of poems, *softly, I speak* (Louisiana Literature Press, 2020), was selected as part of Louisiana Literature Press's chapbook series. To learn more about her current projects, go to byjessicanguyen.com, and follow her @byjessicanguyen on social media.

JAX NTP holds an MFA in creative writing from CSU Long Beach. They currently teach critical thinking, reading, and writing through literature and composition courses at Golden West College, Irvine

Valley College, and Cypress College. Jax is the assistant editor for fiction at *The Offing Magazine*. They were the semi-finalist for Gold Wake Press's Poetry Book Contest and the finalist for Gertrude Press's chapbook contest. Their words have been featured in *Apogee Journal, Berkeley Poetry Review, Hobart Literary Magazine,* and *Queen Mob's Teahouse.*

SIERRA PERRETT is a writer from Vancouver. She is currently pursuing writing at the University of Victoria. Many of her pieces are created when she should be doing something else.

UYEN T. PHAM (Thu Uyên) graduated from Kalamazoo College with a critical ethnic studies major. She's curating a Vietnamese folio for *PANK Magazine* and trying to write: precioussummer. wordpress.com.

ALI RAZ received an MFA in fiction from the University of Notre Dame. Her work has appeared in *3:AM Magazine, Tupelo Quarterly, Occulum, Queen Mob's Teahouse,* and elsewhere. She lives in Los Angeles.

ZODIAC RIVER is a non-binary lesbian author and poet based in Indonesia.

ENCINA ROH is a student and writer from Vancouver, Canada. Formally published at fourteen, she has never strayed far from her love of writing, winning both international and national awards and scholarships for her poetry and critical essays. After obtaining a full ride to college, Encina is currently a law intern and works as a photographer and associate writer for the school paper. She currently holds her position as the founder and president of The Writer's Art, a collective that holds free poetry programs at senior homes and recreational centers to engage the community through writing.

WHITNEY ROMBERG-SASAKI (she/her/hers) is a fourth-generation Japanese American artist and activist. She creates works surrounding themes of self-love, relationships, identity, and healing, especially for queer women of color. In her work, she aims to create a sense of community by organizing events, virtual workshops, and festivals. A California native, Whitney has also been involved in the San Francisco Bay Area and Los Angeles art communities as a featured artist as well as the organizer of Santa Cruz Zine Fest (2016–18). Whitney holds a BA in art from the University of California, Santa Cruz. Along with her art, one of her recent projects has been being one of the creators and hosts of *Building Communi-tea*, a podcast that centers the Asian American millennial experience. To keep up with her projects, check out her Instagram @whitneykittyart, website whitneyromberg.weebly.com, or email whitneyromberg@gmail.com. *Building Communi-tea* (@buildcommunitea) is now available on Spotify, Apple Podcasts, and Anchor.

YURI SAKAKIBARA is a Los Angeles–based designer with a BFA from UCLA's Design | Media Arts program. She is particularly interested in topics pertaining to identity, society, and culture. She often combines the traditional and digital, working in anything from print and typography to 3D-modeling and motion graphics.

MIKI SCHUMACHER is a Filipino-American genderqueer lesbian living in Minneapolis, Minnesota. They believe in the empowering voice inside every writer. You can find them on Twitter @mikischum.

SKR immigrated to the US in the early 2000s. They worked various jobs as a teacher, body worker, energy healer, and occasionally a stripper. Currently they work at a nonprofit that services immigrant communities. SKR is interested in articulating the experiences of living in a queer afab Asian body in a heteronormative patriarchal white supremacist world and all the pleasures, battles, and complexities thereof.

MI OK SONG was born in South Korea, lived in an orphanage for four years, and was adopted at age five to a Dutch American family in New Jersey. She grew up in New Jersey and Rhode Island. Mi Ok attended art school in Virginia, earned her BA in Liberal Arts in Vermont, and earned her MSW at Smith College School for Social Work. She lived in the Bronx, New York, Cambridge, Massachusetts, and South Korea, where she searched for and found her birth family after thirty-six years of estrangement. Mi Ok lived in Korea for two years, teaching English at a university. She returned to live and work in Rhode Island in 2008. Mi Ok currently works in Providence as an LICSW and lives in Warwick with her life partner of nine years and two feline rescues, Frida Calico and Marvin Gray. She conducted over eighty speaking engagements on international adoption issues from 1984–2010. She published thirty poems and several articles and essays from 1990–2000, and since 2008 is currently focusing her creativity on producing drawings with colored pens on gray paper. Mi Ok can be contacted at averyfinecoloredline@gmail.com. Her drawings can be seen at @averyfinecoloredline on Instagram and Facebook.

S.E. SWEA is a Chinese-Malaysian lesbian presently living in George Town, Penang. Swea has previously been published in Issue #6 of *Impossible Archetype*, a journal for LGBTQ poetry edited by Mark Ward.

JANINE SY is an emerging writer that can be found working at a hospital near you. She currently resides in the intersections of her queer and Asian-American identities in the PNW.

LAURA TRAN was born and raised in NYC by Vietnamese refugees. She co-owns and manages XLB, a Chinese restaurant in Portland. She received her BS in women and gender studies from University of Oregon. Along with her partner, she co-directs Meadow, a creative space for women, lgbtqia+, gender non-conforming, and/or POC artists and writers. She supports diverse expressions of creativity and discovered her own in the kitchen. You can visit her at www.xlbpdx.com.

ROSS TUGADE is a lawyer from the Philippines.

KAI TUMANENG is a University of South Florida graduate with a lifelong infatuation for poetry and prose.

ORCHID WEN is a writer and teacher of queer theory. They would like to thank their dog, their grandma, and their therapist.

SYD WESTLEY (they/them) is a queer, mixed-race, non-binary poet from the Bay Area. They are pursuing a BA from Stanford in comparative literature with a focus on marginalized literatures and poetics of America. Westley is a 2019 Lambda Literary Scholarship Recipient & Fellow in Poetry and a 2020 VONA Alumni. They have been published by Stanford University and Dissonance Press.

AYAME WHITFIELD lives by the ocean in Massachusetts and attends Princeton University, where she is majoring in history and hoping to get certificates in visual arts and creative writing. She has had work published in school literary magazines, as well as several online literary journals, including *L'Ephémère Review*, *Subprimal Poetry*, and *Wax Poetry*. When she is not writing, she can be found with her extensive polyhedral dice collection or drinking tea. Find her on Patreon and most social media as @avolitorial.

STEPHANIE WICKHAM is an Australian Born Chinese individual. Her background is half Chinese, half Caucasian, and she identifies as a lesbian.

PEACE WONG is a musician, sound sculptor and singer-songwriter from Hong Kong who currently stations in Taiwan. A current MFA student in Creative Writing at National Dong Hwa University. She released her debut concept album, *About a Stalker*, in late 2018. A collection of intimate bedroom monologues, murmurs, and whispers from an avid onlooker humming to her microphone as a tribute to her online crushes. She also doodles sometimes under a pseudonym, 17ping.

王和平。東華華文文學系研究所創作組在學生。吟歌者，發聲器。暫居台灣，原鄉香港。
二零一八年末推出首張臥室製作音樂專輯及同名小誌《路人崇拜 About a Stalker》，獨立刊物《日常：錄音筆記》。發現在地球難以為繼自此喋喋不休。轄下另有繪圖部精靈王十七平，又名17ping。
Instagram: @peacewong
wongpeace.wixsite.com/aboutastalker

TESSA YANG is a fiction writer from New York State whose work has appeared in *The Cincinnati Review*, *Foglifter*, *Joyland*, and elsewhere. Her flash fiction has been nominated for Best Small Fictions and was included in *Wigleaf*'s Top 50 Very Short Fictions of 2018 and 2019. She received her MFA from Indiana University, where she served as the editor of *Indiana Review*, and currently works as an assistant professor of English at Hartwick College. Find her online at www.tessayang.com, or on Twitter: @ThePtessadactyl.

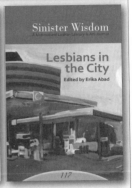

Sinister Wisdom **Back Issues Available**